D1555287

Feminism and Emotion

Also by Susan Mendus

TOLERATION AND THE LIMITS OF LIBERALISM

Feminism and Emotion

Readings in Moral and Political Philosophy

Susan Mendus
Professor of Politics and
Director, Morrell Studies in Toleration
University of York

First published in Great Britain 2000 by
MACMILLAN PRESS LTD
Houndmills, Basingstoke, Hampshire RG21 6XS and London
Companies and representatives throughout the world

A catalogue record for this book is available from the British Library.

ISBN 0–333–80269–1

First published in the United States of America 2000 by
ST. MARTIN'S PRESS, LLC,
Scholarly and Reference Division,
175 Fifth Avenue, New York, N.Y. 10010

ISBN 0–333–80269–1

Library of Congress Cataloging-in-Publication Data have been applied for.

This book is printed on paper suitable for recycling and made from fully managed and sustained forest sources.

10   9   8   7   6   5   4   3   2   1
09   08   07   06   05   04   03   02   01   00

Printed and bound in Great Britain by
Antony Rowe Ltd, Chippenham, Wiltshire

For PPN

Contents

Acknowledgements

With the exception of Chapter 4, this book comprises reworked and revised versions of articles whose original place of publication is given in the final note of each chapter. I would like to thank the following publishers and journals for their permission to reprint copyright material: Cambridge University Press (5, 8, 11), *The Historian* (1), Edinburgh University Press (2), *Journal of Value Inquiry* (3), *Archiv für Recht und Sozialphilosophie* (6), *Journal of Applied Philosophy* (7), *Women's Philosophical Review* (10) and *Philosophical Explorations* (9).

The bulk of the material was written over a period of nearly 15 years and, in that time, I have incurred debts to colleagues and friends too numerous to mention. Specific debts are acknowledged in the essays themselves. Beyond that, I would like to thank the staff and students of the Research School for Social Science at the ANU, Canberra, where I spent an exceptionally happy and productive research term, and the staff and students of the Politics Department at the University of York, especially my colleagues (both past and present) in the political theory sector: Alex Callinicos, David Edwards, John Horton, Duncan Ivison, Matt Matravers and Peter Nicholson.

Peter Nicholson has been my friend and colleague for 20 years. Throughout that time, his support has been unstinting, his advice wise and his patience limitless. I dedicate this book to Peter, with admiration and thanks.

Susan Mendus
University of York

Introduction

The essays gathered together here have been written over a period of nearly 15 years; many have been revised for this volume. Although the essays were written for distinct purposes, they reflect a continuing interest in the role which emotion in general, and love in particular, can play in moral and political philosophy, and the purpose of the book, taken as a whole, is to examine that role and to show how a careful analysis of love can contribute to moral and political theory.

It is a commonplace that the 'great dead' philosophers associated men with reason and women with emotion. It is also a commonplace that many of these philosophers viewed emotion with suspicion, construing it as fickle and capricious. Reason, by contrast, was thought to be constant and reliable, and woman's 'natural' tendency to be guided by emotion was therefore deemed to be something that rendered her untrustworthy in moral life and unsuited for the world of politics. In brief, woman's nature fitted her for a domestic role within the family, where partiality, tenderness and compassion are important and valuable qualities, but by the same token woman's nature rendered her unpredictable in moral matters and wholly unsuited to public or political life, where the impartiality and constancy of reason are of paramount importance. So much is received feminist opinion.

The chapters in this volume attempt to temper that judgement in two ways: first, through a discussion of the work of four 'enlightenment' thinkers – Mary Wollstonecraft, John Stuart Mill, Harriet Taylor and Immanuel Kant – I try to show that the division between reason

1

and emotion was less starkly drawn than is often supposed. Each of these writers argues for the need to understand emotion in a 'moralized' form, and far from construing emotion as distinct from and in opposition to reason, they in fact understand emotion, and especially the emotion of love, as something which, when properly conceptualized, makes essential reference to reason and provides an important complement to it. Moreover, in the case of Mary Wollstonecraft, John Stuart Mill and Harriet Taylor, this insistence on the reconciliation of reason and emotion (the 'moralizing' of emotion as Wollstonecraft calls it) has potentially radical implications for politics. So, my first aim is to show that at least some of the central figures of the enlightenment had a more nuanced understanding of emotion and a more sophisticated account of its relation to reason than is often supposed. My second aim is to show that this 'moralized' understanding of emotion contains important insights for us. In particular, that it has significant consequences for our understanding of the human condition and that it can be deployed in a way that will enrich modern moral and political philosophy.

In the first three chapters of Part I, I discuss the status of love and emotion in the philosophy of Mary Wollstonecraft, John Stuart Mill and Harriet Taylor, and Immanuel Kant. My claim is that each of these writers has a more subtle understanding of emotion than is usually acknowledged, and that each attempts a *rapprochement* between reason and emotion, rather than insisting on the subservience of the latter to the former. I begin with Mary Wollstonecraft, and here I draw upon her correspondence with her lover, Gilbert Imlay. I suggest that, whereas *A Vindication of The Rights of Woman* reveals Wollstonecraft to be deeply suspicious of emotion, her correspondence with Imlay highlights a different side to her character and a different aspect of her philosophical position. For in the correspondence with Imlay, Wollstonecraft emphasizes the importance of 'moralizing' emotion (especially the emotion of love) by bringing it under the control of reason. Her complaint against Imlay was that he either would not or could not do this, and that his failure constituted a distinctively *moral* fault in him. By failing to convert the love of passion into the love of reason Imlay effectively denied that love brings moral obligations with it. However, Mary Wollstonecraft insists that once we accept the love of another we have obligations to that person and must therefore seek to transform mere passion into steady and reliable affection. It was, in her view, a great moral fault in Imlay that he remained a slave to that form of love which is no more than brute passion.

Interesting consequences follow from Mary Wollstonecraft's insistence on the necessity of moralizing love. One is that, although she is an enlightenment thinker, she does not decry the significance of love in particular, or of emotion in general. On the contrary, she insists that once it has been properly understood and tempered by reason, it is central to morality. The second consequence is that, having emphasized the possibility and importance of moralized love, she goes on to draw political conclusions which are more radical than is usually acknowledged. In particular, her insistence on women's 'special' and distinctive qualities, when read in conjunction with her argument for the need to moralize emotion, can be seen to have the effect of challenging the public/private distinction and of questioning the priority given to the public arena over the private.

The chapter on John Stuart Mill and Harriet Taylor pursues this theme, and here I note that for Mill, as for Wollstonecraft, it was an event in his own life which led to the insistence that emotion and reason should not be separated, but rather should be seen as operating in conjunction with one another. Having been brought up in a strict and unrelenting regime of education, Mill succumbed, at the age of 20, to a 'mental crisis' which is poignantly described in his *Autobiography*. That crisis consisted of a loss of faith in all he had previously believed in and thought worthwhile, and it abated only when he came into contact with people who, as he saw it, could make good what was lacking in his own logical and rational nature. Thus, by his own account, Mill's emergence from the mental crisis took the form of a growing awareness that reason alone was not enough, and that a person who knew only the dictates of reason was 'one-eyed'. Therefore, to make good what was lacking in his own temperament and intellect, he sought the company of people of a more 'intuitive' or 'emotional' cast of mind than his own. Chief amongst these were poets and creative writers such as Samuel Taylor Coleridge, Thomas Carlyle and, most importantly, Harriet Taylor. These people, he tells us, made him aware that reason must be complemented by intuition, logic by imagination and proof by insight. Although Mill and Harriet Taylor do not share Wollstonecraft's suspicion of unmoralized love as a 'stalking mischief', they nevertheless concur with her in thinking that reason and emotion must be combined in any adequate account of morality. Moreover, this insistence on the complementarity of reason and emotion can again be seen as having radical political implications beyond those normally attributed to Mill and Taylor. All three writers, then, insist on the moralization of love and, in all three cases, that insistence suggests a radical interpretation of their political views.

The third chapter discusses Immanuel Kant's understanding of love and concentrates on the distinction he draws between practical and pathological love in *Groundwork for a Metaphysic of Morals*. Although Kant is often portrayed as an enemy of love (a 'misamorist'), and although that interpretation is certainly not without warrant, it is nevertheless important to understand precisely why Kant was suspicious of love, and against what form of love his suspicion was directed. In 'The Practical and the Pathological' I argue that Kant's deep motivation is a desire to render moral assessment immune to the vagaries of luck and contingency. Because love, when understood 'pathologically' (as a brute emotion), is not under the control of the will, it is unfair that anyone should be assessed morally by reference to their ability to display it. Therefore (and again), love must be 'moralized', or brought under the control of the will, if it is to form a proper component in the moral assessment of the individual. And it is part of Kant's aim to show that love can be so moralized.

Judith Shklar has suggested that Kant's moral philosophy is, at root, a philosophy of the ordinary person: 'anyone can in principle aspire to become a Kantian good person. It requires no special gifts of intelligence, beauty, wealth or good luck.'[1] Read in this way, the distinction between practical and pathological love is one that aims to ensure that even the person of cold heart, in whom nature has implanted little natural sympathy, can nevertheless be a morally good person. Like Wollstonecraft, Kant emphasizes the importance of bringing emotion under the control of reason and thus rendering it a proper object of moral assessment. Love which springs solely from inclination has indeed no moral worth, but love which is brought under the control of reason and thus rendered reliable and consistent is the mark of a morally good person. Moreover, and importantly, in urging this moralization of love, Kant is insisting on something more than simply cold deeds done for the sake of duty. He is urging the cultivation of emotions such as kindness (not merely kind acts, but genuine kindness), and I suggest that the arguments of his *Lectures on Ethics* build upon the distinction between practical and pathological love drawn in *Groundwork* and indicate that emotion, far from being excluded from his moral philosophy, is in fact a presupposition of it. The first three chapters therefore aim to show that at least some enlightenment philosophers held a more sophisticated and nuanced view of emotion than has usually been attributed to them.

In the chapters which follow I attempt to draw out some of the implications of this moralization of love, and I argue that modern moral and political philosophy can be enriched by it. The final two chapters in Part I consider how a moralized conception of love can inform moral philosophy, while the chapters in Part II discuss the wider political implications of taking love seriously. Yet more generally, the chapters pursue two themes: first, by drawing on feminist philosophy, they note the ways in which our lives are subject to luck, chance and contingency; second, by drawing on the enlightenment philosophers discussed in the first three chapters, they ask how the moralization of love can reflect and perhaps even mitigate the worst effects of that contingency.

'Time and Chance' begins by noting feminist suspicion of Kant's moral philosophy. As has already been pointed out, feminist moral and political philosophers are often unsympathetic to enlightenment understandings of the relationship between reason and emotion, at least in their traditional and stereotypical form. However, feminists are also sensitive to the contingency of life and to the ways in which people may be at the mercy of luck and circumstance. These two insights are connected, because it is often thought that a recognition of the contingency of life sits ill with a form of moral philosophy which emphasizes individual autonomy and the possibility of control over our lives and actions. Recognition of the ubiquity of luck has therefore prompted many feminists to reject Kantianism in favour of a more contextualized conception of moral and political philosophy, one that gives lower priority to autonomy and higher priority to a conception of human beings as vulnerable, needy and (often) unable to control their own lives. However, and somewhat ironically, in doing this feminists run the risk of neglecting the deep motivation which, I claim, lies at the heart of Kant's project – the motivation to secure the moral realm from the operation of luck. The distinction between practical and pathological love and the doctrine of the core self are, I suggest, both introduced by Kant in an attempt to claim for the agent some moral immunity from the operation of chance or fortune. It is therefore the recognition, not the denial, of contingency which informs his project. Additionally, the doctrine of the core self is one which aspires to justify morality by providing reasons for thinking that, whatever differences divide us, we are all, in the end, moral beings. Therefore, in emphasizing difference, feminist theorists need to be alert to the possibility that they are also, and simultaneously, robbing their moral and political theory of the tools necessary to justify morality itself. In both these respects, the concerns which motivate feminist theory are also concerns which motivate Kant's moral theory.

Where 'Time and Chance' concentrates on the ways in which moral theory can best reflect our status as vulnerable and needy creatures, and argues that this aspiration lies at the very heart of the Kantian project, 'Marital Faithfulness' argues that modern moral philosophy must take seriously the need to moralize emotions, and especially the emotion of love. Here I discuss the status of the marriage promise as a promise to love, and I argue that we can make sense of that promise only if we refrain from seeing it as a promise to feel a certain way. In the chapter on Mary Wollstonecraft I noted that her objection to Imlay was that he refused to convert the love of passion into the love of reason. In other words, he refused to see that love brings obligations with it, and that to fail to love is therefore to fail morally. Similarly here I argue that this moralized understanding of love is central to our ability to make sense of the marriage promise, which is properly understood as a commitment, not as a promise to feel a certain way. So the moralization of emotion is an important component in our understanding of the moral ideal of marriage.

The chapters which are presented in Part II concentrate on the political consequences which might follow from a moralized understanding of love, and the first chapter of Part II ('To Have and to Hold') is the political analogue of the last chapter of Part I ('Marital Faithfulness'). Whereas the latter chapter discussed the morality of the marriage promise, and the status of promises to love, this chapter discusses the public status of marriage and, in particular, its status as a legal contract between two people. Individuals who marry characteristically think of themselves (at least in modern, western societies) as making a public statement of their private commitment to one another. They are, however, also entering into a legal contract, sanctioned and controlled by the laws of the state. Thus, marriage is an interesting case study for both feminists and political philosophers generally: it straddles the divide between public and private and, for that very reason, raises questions about the connection between the private motivation for entering into marriage and the legal and political status attained thereby.

'Marital Faithfulness' made some suggestions about the potentially misleading consequences of interpreting marriage at the personal level as a matter of raw emotion, or of what Kant would call 'pathological love'; 'To Have and to Hold' makes some suggestions about the potentially misleading consequences of interpreting marriage at the political level as a kind of contract. Additionally, I suggest that the kind of love which is involved in marriage is one which is distinct from, and not reducible to, the contract model. Thus, it is not simply that there are two facets to marriage: a private or personal facet, which prioritizes love, and a public or legal facet, which prioritizes contract. Rather, the ideal of love which is implicit in marriage at the personal level is inconsistent with the bargaining model which lies at the heart of contract, and indeed at the heart of much liberal political theory. For in so far as love, in a personal sense, involves a renunciation of the language of contract, it is an ideal which conflicts with the public or legal understanding of marriage as essentially a contractual arrangement.

The next chapter, 'Different Voices, Still Lives', is the political analogue of 'Time and Chance'. In 'Time and Chance' I emphasized the moral importance of acknowledging the contingency of life and our susceptibility to luck. In 'Different Voices, Still Lives' I discuss the political implications of that recognition and argue for an interpretation of the ethics of care which highlights vulnerability and contingency rather than the activity of caring. I suggest that emphasis on the activity of caring is potentially damaging for women, particularly if it is extended to the political realm, where it can endorse a requirement of unlimited sacrifice to the needs of others, and thus compound rather than alleviate the problems women encounter as carers. By contrast, an interpretation of the ethics of care which takes human vulnerability as central can largely avoid both these problems.

Our nature as needy creatures, and our vulnerability to luck, is discussed more generally in 'Tragedy, Moral Conflict and Liberalism'. Here I consider the resources which liberal political philosophy has for coping with vulnerability and accommodating the conflict which is consequent upon it. I note that liberalism springs from a recognition of the facts of conflict, and attempts to deal with those facts by instituting justice at the political level. Social justice aims to mitigate the worst effects of brute bad luck. This strategy, although admirable in many ways, can ultimately result in a denial of our nature as vulnerable creatures. It nurtures the belief that in a just society people can properly be held responsible for the misfortunes that befall them, and that, if politics goes well, bad luck can be eliminated. I argue that there is a considerable irony in this approach for, in the end, it generates a new and distinctively modern form of tragedy – one that arises not from our susceptibility to the operations of fate, but rather from the very belief that we can be rendered immune from those operations.

The relationship between tragedy and modern liberalism is discussed further in 'Out of the Doll's House', which concentrates on the way in which liberal invocation of autonomy can exaggerate both the extent to which we do in fact control our own lives and the desirability of attaining that control. Feminist insights about our status as vulnerable and needy creatures, constrained by circumstance, are deployed in order to highlight the dangers inherent in a form of liberalism which places too much emphasis on the value of autonomy understood as authorship of one's own life. Moreover, the potentially tragic consequences of this understanding of autonomy are, I argue, connected to the emphasis which such a conception of autonomy places on the separateness of persons. That emphasis can plausibly be sustained only by ignoring the role which love plays in blurring the distinction between self and others. In short, then, feminist claims about neediness and vulnerability, when taken together with an understanding of love as something more than brute emotion, can deepen our understanding of ourselves and thus of moral and political philosophy.

The final two chapters ('Strangers in Paradise' and 'The Importance of Love in Rawls's Theory of Justice') concentrate on the conception of the self which should inform moral and political philosophy. Both chapters argue for a dynamic rather than a static conception of the self, but where 'Strangers in Paradise' insists that a dynamic conception is needed in order to resolve tensions at the heart of radical feminism, 'The Importance of Love' insists that a dynamic conception is needed in order to resolve tensions at the heart of liberalism. Thus, 'Strangers in Paradise' focuses on the uneasy alliance between radical feminism and moral conservatism, and argues that in order to avoid charges of moralism or political conservatism, feminists must see the self as capable of change. In particular, insistence on woman's distinctive nature as caring and compassionate threatens to deliver political conclusions which will be damaging to feminist aspirations rather than supportive of them, and the way to avoid that threat is to understand the self as dynamic rather than static.

Similarly, in 'The Importance of Love', I argue that the project of Rawlsian liberalism can best be fulfilled by noting that the self is capable of change, and moreover that such change is often prompted by love. Rawls's task in Part III of *A Theory of Justice* is to explain moral motivation and, in particular, to defend his claim that acting morally well is congruent with the agent's own good. Rawls's critics have declared this ambition to be unattainable, and Rawls himself has concluded that the attempt to demonstrate such congruence has committed him to an objectionably Kantian metaphysics. However, I argue that if we take seriously the ways in which love for others can alter our projects and prompt revision in our conception of our own good (and thus in our understanding of ourselves), the problem of moral motivation can be satisfactorily resolved.

What motivates these chapters, then, is a desire to reconcile the insights of modern feminist theory with the insights of enlightenment philosophy generally, and modern liberalism in particular. Through discussion of Mary Wollstonecraft, John Stuart Mill, Harriet Taylor and Immanuel Kant, I argue that at least some enlightenment thinkers were more sympathetic to the role of emotion in morality than is usually supposed. I also claim that their emphasis on emotion, and on the importance of moralizing emotion, can be read as a deep recognition of human vulnerability and susceptibility to luck.

Moreover, that same recognition is central to, indeed definitive of, much modern feminist theory. It is, I argue, at the heart of feminist commitment to the ethics of care, which is best understood as an ethical theory which gives centrality to a conception of the self as inextricably intertwined with others and dependent upon them for flourishing. Negatively, the acknowledgement of this interdependence is important if we are to avoid distorting our understanding of conflict and of tragedy. More positively, however, the acknowledgement of interdependence is also central to the success of modern liberal political theory. Cases of love highlight the fact that we are dependent on others, but also serve to emphasize that the dependence can be constitutive of our good, rather than destructive of our autonomy.

I am conscious that these chapters, which were written separately and over a long period of time, are not always consistent one with another. However, they were all written from a persistent desire to demonstrate that love has an indispensable role to play in modern moral and political philosophy. However, that role is not the one explicitly identified by care theorists. Rather it is the one implicitly acknowledged by (some) enlightenment thinkers of the past and (some) liberal theorists of the present. My attempts to demonstrate this are preliminary and tentative, but I hope that they will none the less provide food for further thought.

Part I
The Morality of Love

1
When the Kissing Had to Stop: Passion in the Thought of Mary Wollstonecraft

There are, we are told, two Mary Wollstonecrafts: one who loved, and one who was contemptuous of love.[1] Mary Wollstonecraft, the feminist intellectual and author of *A Vindication of the Rights of Woman*, declared love to be 'a stalking mischief'. 'Love,' she insisted, 'from its very nature must be transitory . . . friendship or indifference inevitably succeeds love.' And a good thing too, for 'in order to fulfil the duties of life, and to be able to pursue with vigour the various employments which form the moral character, a master and mistress of a family ought not to continue to love each other with passion. They ought not to indulge those emotions which disturb the order of society, and engross the thoughts that should otherwise be employed.'[2] For this Mary Wollstonecraft, love is not merely transitory, capricious and unreliable at the individual level, it is also a sign of moral weakness and the harbinger of vast and unspeakable social disorder. Moreover, the disorder was not confined to the home itself but, if left unchecked, would spread through society generally. Sensualists she wrote, 'pig together in the same bed chamber' and acquire vices which 'render the body weak whilst they effectually prevent the acquisition of any delicacy of mind.'[3] Like a serpent, love nestles in the bosom waiting to strike and inject its venom into the individual, and thus through society as a whole. The only antidote to love is reason, and *A Vindication of the Rights of Woman* is an extended paean of praise to the reliability and constancy of reason, against the moral degeneracy of love.

However, this portrait of Mary Wollstonecraft as sexual prude and tireless advocate of the death of passion fits ill with the biographical facts. The Mary Wollstonecraft who, in her writings, could speak so scathingly of love was also the Mary Wollstonecraft who, in life, was infatuated to the point of suicide by love for Gilbert Imlay. When, in 1797, at the age of 38, she died of septicaemia contracted in child-birth, her husband, William Godwin, published his *Memoirs of the Author of 'The Rights of Woman'*, and outraged polite society with a graphic account of his wife's emotional and sexual life. *The European Magazine* referred to Godwin's book as 'the history of a philosophi-cal wanton' and was sure that it would be read 'with detestation by everyone attached to the interests of religion and morality'. *The Anti-Jacobin* indexed the book under 'Prostitution: see Mary Woll-stonecraft', and in 1801 the following poem was published, which gives an indication of how Mary Wollstonecraft's life was perceived, whatever her works might say:

> William hath penned a waggon-load of stuff
> And Mary's life at last he needs must write,
> Thinking her whoredoms were not known enough,
> Till fairly printed off in black and white.
> With wondrous glee and pride, this simple wight
> Her brothel feats of wantonness sets down;
> Being her spouse, he tells with huge delight,
> How oft she cuckolded the silly clown,
> And lent, O lovely piece!, herself to half the town.[4]

Intellectually she may have been the champion of reason over passion, but in her life she was a tragic and romantic heroine with whom feminists were ashamed to be associated. Saying publicly what others thought privately, the Victorian feminist Harriet Martineau observed that 'women of the Wollstonecraft order . . . do infinite mis-chief, and, for my part, I do not wish to have anything to do with them. She is neither a safe example, nor a successful champion of Woman and her Rights.'[5]

Crudely put, the problem was (and to some extent still is) that Mary Wollstonecraft appeared not to be very good at practising what she preached. Rejecting sensualism and advocating the death of passion in *A Vindication*, she nevertheless had an ill-judged affair with Henry Fuseli, an illegitimate child by Gilbert Imlay and a mar-riage to William Godwin which was precipitated by her calling upon him (an unusual and improper reversal of the proprieties of eighteenth-century courtship). She was seen as damaging the cause of women by the excesses of her personal life, and Godwin only inflamed matters by making public the indelicate details of her numerous sexual liaisons. If, in her writings, the kissing had to stop early, in her life it seemed never to stop at all. Moreover, this apparent conflict between theory and practice continues to be a source of embarrassment for modern biographers of Mary Wollstonecraft. Claire Tomalin (writing in 1974) takes Godwin to task for emphasizing Wollstonecraft's personal life to the detriment of her philosophical ideas, thereby 'diminishing and distorting her real importance'. By presenting her as a romantic and tragic heroine he may, says Tomalin, 'have been giving the truth as he wanted to see it, but he was very far from serving the cause she had believed in. He made no attempt to discuss her intellectual development and he was unwilling to consider the validity of her feminist ideals in any detail.'[6] For modern biographers, as for Wollstonecraft's contemporaries, there is indelicacy and embarrassment in the detailed raking over of her personal life, and that embarrassment is a direct result of her perceived inability to live up to the moral standards which, in her writings, she pressed so fervently on others.

In this chapter, I have two aims: the first is to reconcile Mary Wollstonecraft the woman with Mary Wollstonecraft the philosopher. Despite appearances to the contrary, there is, I believe, no contradiction between the rejection of passion advocated in *A Vindication* and the unbearably poignant, even tragic, details of Mary Wollstonecraft's emotional and sexual life. On the contrary, the humiliating course of her relationship with Gilbert Imlay is a proof of all she feared and warned against as author of *A Vindication*. It is not, in my view, too much of an exaggeration to say that in her affair with Gilbert Imlay, Wollstonecraft lived out the terrible truth of the theory which she had presented in *A Vindication*. That theory is that passion, love, sensuality, is a 'stalking mischief', which will destroy all in its path unless it is moralized via the operation of reason. So Imlay nearly destroyed her. Of course, he protested his love throughout, but this 'love' was none other than the stalking mischief – the love of passion and not the love of reason. All her efforts to convert the one into the other failed, and Imlay turned out to be the sensualist *par excellence*. In her relationship with Imlay, Mary

Wollstonecraft lived the nightmare of loving a man whom she came to recognize as profoundly and irremediably immoral, and this experience confirmed her belief in the necessity of moralizing love by bringing it under the control of reason. In short, her life and her philosophy, far from being in contradiction, were poignantly harmonious.

Moreover, Wollstonecraft's insistence on the *moral* dimension of love was a prelude to her insistence on its *political* dimension. Her conviction that love must be moralized rested on the belief that it serves as the foundation of political order. If, at the political level, we expect people to reject self-interest in favour of the common good, then we must acknowledge that the family is the natural arena in which such qualities of restraint will be learned. It follows that the home and the marriage which are based on unmoralized passion, will not be ones in which political virtues such as self-restraint will be acquired. And so, the sensualist is not merely a moral reprobate, but a political danger, for he is blind and deaf to those principles on which alone a good political order can be founded. My second aim, therefore, is to discuss the political dimension of love (the politics of passion) as it appears in Mary Wollstonecraft's writings. I begin, however, with the attempted reconciliation of life and works.

Passion and morality

In order to reconcile Mary Wollstonecraft's life with her philosophy, we must first understand exactly what her philosophy is and, most importantly, the background against which it was written. The theory which Mary Wollstonecraft puts forward in *A Vindication* can be stated fairly briskly. It is that women, like men, are first and foremost rational creatures and that the possibility of moral goodness consists in the development of their rationality:

> Reason is, consequentially, the simple power of improvement; or, more properly speaking, of discerning truth . . . considering woman as a whole, let it be what it will, instead of a part of man, the inquiry is whether she have reason or not. If she have, which, for the moment, I take for granted, she was not created merely to be the solace of man, and the sexual should not destroy the human character.[7]

However, although the theory is easily stated, its implications are far-reaching. By insisting on the essential sameness of men and women, Wollstonecraft is opposing a long tradition of philosophical and 'common-sense' thinking, according to which woman's nature is quite distinct and different from man's nature. The *bête noir* in this context is, of course her contemporary, Jean-Jacques Rousseau, but he is far from being the only adherent to the cause, and in the early chapters of *A Vindication* Wollstonecraft devotes a great deal of time to detailing the common opinion of women in the eyes of 'great men'. She is, moreover, especially vituperative in cataloguing the adverse effect which that common opinion had on women's education. As Tomaselli notes:

> Wollstonecraft took to task political legislators, parents, preachers, schoolmasters and mistresses, tutors and governesses, and authors such as Rousseau, Dr Gregory, James Fordyce and Lord Chesterfield. She found fault with them all. The *Vindication* was dedicated to the former Bishop of Autin, Charles Maurice de Talleyrand-Perigord, who called on her during a visit to London shortly afterwards. She upbraided him for not treating men and women equally in his *Rapport sur l'instruction publique* . . . a revised constitution, she urged, had to do justice to the whole of the human race and hence recognize the rights of woman as well as man.[8]

Thus, in urging the essential sameness of men and women, Mary Wollstonecraft was not uttering a banal and obvious truth, but putting forward a thesis which seemed controversial to many, and straightforwardly preposterous to some. Chief amongst the latter was the political philosopher, Jean-Jacques Rousseau who, in *Emile*, in *La Nouvelle Héloïse* and elsewhere had provided a detailed account of the different natures of men and women. In *Emile* Rousseau writes:

> A perfect man and a perfect woman should be no more alike in mind than in face . . . the man should be strong and active, the woman should be weak and passive; the one must have both the power and the will; it is enough that the other should offer little resistance.[9]

From these 'natural' differences between men and women spring both moral differences and political differences, differences which determine the place in society appropriate for men and women respectively. What, then, are these natural differences? Chief amongst them is woman's passionate nature which, according to Rousseau, distinguishes her from man and makes it not merely desirable, but imperative that there be a double standard of sexual conduct, distinct patterns of education and inequalities in man-made laws. He writes: 'women do wrong to complain of the inequality of man-made laws; this inequality is not of man's making, or at any rate it is not the result of mere prejudice but of reason.' Without those inequalities of law, woman's boundless sexual passion would lead to grave disorder in the state, for women have a power of stimulating men's passion far in excess of man's power of satisfying them and thus, if women were treated equally with men, 'the result would be the destruction of both and the men, tyrannized over by the women, would at last become their victims, and would be dragged to their death without the least chance of escape.'[10]

Spoken in the late twentieth century, these claims may appear simply absurd, pieces of academic archaeology, or unfair and faintly comic sticks with which to beat the great dead philosophers. But they are more than that. Rousseau's views reflected contemporary opinion about women, but they also influenced the structure of his political theory, notably his claims about the principles on which societies should be organized. From the premiss that men and women are naturally different, Rousseau developed a theory of politics which separated men and women into different spheres of activity – the men dominating in the public or political realm, while women ruled in the private or domestic sphere. In so far as modern theorists accept the structure of Rousseau's political theory (and many do), they may also be implicitly acknowledging his views about the different nature of men and women. I shall say more about this possibility later. For now, however, my focus is the reconciliation of Mary Wollstonecraft the woman and Mary Wollstonecraft the philosopher.

A Vindication is, in large part, an extended critique of Rousseau's claim that men and women are by nature different. Against Rousseau, Wollstonecraft argues that both men and women are essentially rational creatures, that virtue or moral goodness is the same for both, and that both are entitled to equal political rights and educational opportunities. Specifically, and since we are rational creatures, virtue consists in bringing the passions under the control of reason. And since we are the same, whether men or women, this injunction holds for both men and women alike. If women are unable to control passion, this is not, she thinks, because of their different nature, but because their education is inadequate and because they have been taught from an early age that their only purpose is to please men. What Rousseau attributes to 'nature', Wollstonecraft attributes to the corrupting effect of a narrow and inadequate education. She writes:

> Women ought to endeavour to purify their heart; but can they do so when their uncultivated understandings make them entirely dependent on their senses for employment and amusement, when no noble pursuit sets them above the vanities of the day, or enables them to curb the wild emotions that agitate a reed over which every passing breeze has power? . . . Weakness may excite tenderness, and gratify the arrogant pride of man; but the lordly caresses of a protector will not gratify a noble mind that pants for, and deserves to be respected. Fondness is a poor substitute for friendship.[11]

This quotation – and there are many similar ones in *A Vindication* – suggests a distinction between the love of passion (or fondness), which is transitory, and the love of friendship, which is reliable and has its foundation in reason. For Wollstonecraft, the morality of love lay in the possibility of converting the one into the other. Importantly, it did not consist in the denial of sexual passion, but rather in the firm resolve to convert that passion into the love of friendship. 'The most holy band of society is friendship,' she wrote,[12] and 'it has been well said, by a shrewd satirist, "that rare as true love is, true friendship is rarer".'[13] In her affair with Gilbert Imlay, she was soon to discover how right she was.

Mary Wollstonecraft first met Imlay in 1793, the year after the publication of *A Vindication*. During the months of June, July and August of that year she lived in Neuilly, France, where he visited her regularly. In August 1793 she conceived a child and, on discovering this, she returned to Paris and to Imlay, writing: 'You can scarcely imagine with what pleasure I anticipate the day when we are almost to begin to live together.' Perhaps he could, for he left almost immediately for Le Havre 'on business' and their subsequent relationship, documented in her letters to him, is a pitiful tale of her attempts to sustain his interest and his attempts to flee from her. Her letters to him are almost unbearably self-abasing: love for Gilbert Imlay transformed Mary Wollstonecraft from a strong and independent-minded woman into a pitiful, submissive, pleading wretch, governed to the point of obsession by a desire to please a man who was, even in the opinion of his friends, an unreliable dolt. The following letter, written in July 1795, gives the flavour of the affair:

> Do not tell me that you are happier without us. Will you not come to us in Switzerland? Ah why do you not love us with more sentiment? Why are you a creature of such sympathy, that the warmth of your feelings, or rather quickness of your senses, hardens your heart? It is my misfortune that my imagination is perpetually shading your defects and lending you charms, whilst the grossness of your senses makes you overlook graces in me that only dignity of mind and the sensibility of an expanded heart can give.[14]

Again and again she writes to him in this way, her letters vacillating uneasily between irritation at his unreliability, distress at his callousness, and humiliation in the face of his clear disregard for her. But if her contemporaries drew from all this the conclusion that she was a 'loose woman', the judgement of twentieth-century feminist writers has been hardly less sanctimonious – and not without interest from a philosophical as well as a biographical point of view. Valerie Bryson writes:

> In print she often seemed a prim moralist . . . in real life, however, she was to find such precepts unworkable, and many a modern feminist whose heart refuses to obey the dictates of logic and political correctness will empathise with her experience of her unhappy love affairs and sympathise with the conflict between love and reason articulated in her private correspondence.[15]

Claire Tomalin concurs, claiming that Mary Wollstonecraft's views on love were 'wholly altered' by her affair with Imlay; Eleanor Flexnor too identifies the conflict between Mary Wollstonecraft's emotional needs and her intellectual views as *the* dilemma of modern woman. Later feminists, says Flexnor, 'have emphasised her radical demands for education and broader opportunities for women, while they have omitted or drastically de-emphasised her longing for family life and happiness.'[16]

In these judgements there is often a barely repressed sense of triumph at the prospect of an intellectual woman finally getting her emotional and sexual come-uppance. Mary Wollstonecraft was too clever by half, but in the end even her intellect bowed to love and she was forced to acknowledge that the female heart has its reasons which reason knows not of. But did it really, as Claire Tomalin insists, 'wholly alter' her views on love? I think not. The letters to Imlay certainly express her sexual attraction to him, and their poignancy is at least partly derived from the fact that her love for him was unrequited, but there is more. Her disappointment in him springs as much from the fact that he failed her morally as from the fact that he rejected her sexually, and it is this aspect of the affair on which I will now concentrate.

From the beginning, what was unsatisfactory about Mary Wollstonecraft's relationship with Gilbert Imlay was his unwillingness, or inability, to 'moralize' his love by bringing it under the control of reason and converting it from a sexual passion into a more steady affection. In one of her earliest letters to him (before he began fleeing from her) she writes:

> Good night! God bless you! Sterne says that is equal to a kiss – yet I would rather give you the kiss into the bargain, glowing with gratitude and affection to you. I like the word affection, because it signifies something habitual; and we are soon to meet, to try whether we have mind enough to keep our hearts warm.[17]

In this letter we can discern the initial hope that emotion would be converted into affection, and that passion would become something steady and reliable, something 'habitual'. Far from a conflict between passion and reason, Mary Wollstonecraft insists upon the one being a preliminary to the other. Later in their affair, when she had pursued him vainly from port to port and from town to town, she wrote:

> Why do you not attach those tender emotions around the idea of home, which even now dim my eyes? This alone is affection – everything else is only humanity, electrified by sympathy.[18]

And again:

> The tremendous power who formed this heart must have foreseen
> that, in a world in which self-interest, in various shapes, is the
> principal mobile, I had little chance of escaping misery. To the fiat
> of fate I submit. I am content to be wretched; but I will not be
> contemptible. Of me you have no cause to complain, but for
> having had too much regard for you – for having expected a
> degree of permanent happiness, when you only sought for a
> momentary gratification.[19]

These references to the importance of a reliable and habitual love
persist throughout her letters to Imlay, and suggest that what went
wrong in her relationship with him was not, as the commentators
insist, that she here encountered a conflict between reason and
emotion, but rather that Imlay presented himself to her as a sensualist – as one who was either unwilling or unable to moralize his love.
Where her love for him was moralized into affection, his love for her
was simply a fleeting passion. And this mattered to her both personally and philosophically.

It would, of course, be absurd to deny that there is also in the letters
the raw cry of a woman who cannot accept that she is not loved.
There is, additionally, a huge amount of emotional blackmail. Several
times in the letters to Imlay she threatened to kill herself, and twice
she proved that these threats were not idle, but throughout the letters
there is also a plea for the moral necessity of a reconciliation between
love and reason, and the charge against Imlay is that he is deaf to
the demands of reason and moves like an animal from one mistress
to another. For Mary Wollstonecraft the future of mankind depended
crucially upon the possibility of moralizing love and turning it
into something reliable and habitual. In so far as there is a conflict
between reason and emotion, it is not a conflict *for her*: it is a conflict which she perceived and sought to resolve in the life of Gilbert
Imlay.

Commentators are therefore mistaken in claiming that Wollstonecraft's view of love was wholly altered by her affair with Imlay.
On the contrary, her view of Imlay was wholly altered by her affair
with him, but she was never deflected from the belief that it matters

both morally and politically that love shall be more than and different from a transitory sensation or fleeting sexual passion.

The politics of passion

Why does it matter that reason should control passion and transform appetite into steady affection? The most basic reason, as we have seen, is that human beings are by nature rational creatures and it is therefore a denial of that rationality (and a denial of one's nature) to allow passion to reign.

A second reason, highlighted in the letters to Imlay, it that the control of passion is a moral requirement. Since we are rational creatures, our moral goodness consists in the exercise and development of that rationality, and it is a moral failing, exemplified in high degree by Imlay, to disregard rationality. However, the rule of reason over passion is also a political necessity, because social order and political peace depend crucially upon the operation of reason rather than passion. In the case of men, this claim was well established, but for women it needed to be defended, and in *A Vindication* Mary Wollstonecraft provides an elaborate account of why the education of women to a state of reason is of supreme importance for social and political harmony.

In her article 'The Disorder of Women', Carole Pateman notes that the traditional association of women with passion, and the denial that women are rational creatures, has led directly to their exclusion from political society. Pateman writes:

In the 17th century individuals began to be seen as rational beings, born free and equal to each other and as individuals who create their social relationships and institutions for themselves. Political institutions, in particular, began to be seen as, properly, based on convention – on contract, consent and agreement. But do all individuals have the requisite nature or natural capacities? Or are there some who lack, or cannot develop, the capacities required for participation in public life? If these individuals exist their nature will appear as a threat to social life and there has been wide agreement that women are dangerous for this very reason. Women, by virtue of their natures are a disorder in the state.[20]

Woman's alleged lack of rationality, and her association with the emotional, renders her unsuitable for political life, and her proper place is therefore within the home, where the demands of love rather than of reason are paramount. Thus, woman's nature dictates her place in society (or, rather, her place outside society and in the home). There are two possible feminist responses to the exclusion of women from political life: the standard, liberal feminist response is simply to insist that nature is no more destiny for women than it is for men, that women, when educated, may develop reason with which to temper passion, and that they should therefore be accorded all the usual political rights extended to men. So far, this sounds like the Wollstonecraft strategy. However, there is also a second response, and there are hints of this too in Mary Wollstonecraft. This approach rejects the contention that women's passionate nature necessarily presents a threat to the state and argues, on the contrary, that politics or public life, should find room for love and compassion (women's qualities) as well as for justice and reason (men's qualities).

Sometimes Mary Wollstonecraft appears to want to have this particular piece of cake and eat it too. She argues consistently for the importance of equal rights for women, based on her initial premise that both men and women are essentially rational creatures, but then she goes on to maintain that rationality will manifest itself differently in men and in women. Many commentators have identified this as the Achilles' heel in her writings. They interpret her as arguing that although women should have equal political rights, they will not in fact exercise them, preferring to remain within the domestic sphere and to fulfil their traditional roles as child-carers and home-makers. There is however a different, and more radical, interpretation of Wollstonecraft's position, and I will end by considering it briefly.

In insisting upon the differentiation of men's and women's contribution to politics, Mary Wollstonecraft may be interpreted, not as renouncing or qualifying her feminism, but as raising a question which is of the first importance for modern feminism. That question is, 'Why is the home itself not part of the political domain?' As we have seen, philosophers such as Rousseau, who urged that men's and women's natures were different, also, and thereby, distinguished between two spheres – a political and private sphere. The claim that for woman nature was destiny meant that for woman the proper area of operation must be the home and not the state. Thus the alleged 'disorder' of women leads to the division between public and private spheres. By casting doubt on the former distinction, Mary Wollstonecraft also casts doubt on the latter and, by implication, urges the politicization of marriage and of the family. This she does in a number of ways, most of which are merely alluded to rather than spelled out in any detail.

Her explicit claim, as we have seen, is that the home is the arena in which virtues of citizenship are to be learned, and she raises the pertinent (and now familiar) question of how those virtues can be learned if either the mother is uneducated or the father is a mere sensualist. More profoundly, and as we saw in discussing her relationship with Imlay, she wishes to see the family, and specifically marriage, not as a relationship sustained by love or sexual passion, but rather as a kind of contract in which the impetuosity and unreliability of sexual feeling will soon be replaced by or transformed into a more steady and reliable 'affection' founded on moral principle. In November 1795 she wrote to Imlay:

> You can tell me that I shall judge more coolly of your mode of acting some time hence. But is it not possible that passion clouds your reason as much as it does mine? And ought you not to doubt whether those principles are so 'exalted', as you term them, which only lead to your own gratification? In other words, whether it would be just to have no principle of action but that of following your own inclination, trampling on the affection you have fostered, and the expectation you have excited?[21]

For Mary Wollstonecraft, sexual love does not come alone, but brings moral obligation with it, and if that moral obligation is to be fulfilled, there must be a resolve to transform sexual passion into 'steady affection'.

But how does all this generate a *politics*, as distinct from merely a *morality* of passion? To answer this question we must look again at what Wollstonecraft was against – namely an understanding of marriage as essentially a matter of love, where love is understood in the romantic or sexual sense. If marriage is interpreted in this way, then it stands opposed to the political realm, for the political realm is a

realm in which there are rights, obligations, contracts and entitlements. If contracts are broken or obligations not discharged, then the
whole might of the law may be brought down upon the offender,
but where marriage is understood as essentially a matter of love, then
it lies largely outside these political or public constraints. To understand a relationship as a relationship of love is precisely to assert that
one will not, in general, speak the language of legal and political right
within it. Thus, by marrying, a woman relinquishes political power,
particularly power against her husband, and acquires instead the
status of 'wife' which is, by definition, a status in which considerations of justice are replaced by considerations of love. The decision
to marry for love is therefore the decision to put oneself, in so far as
one is a wife, largely outside the interest of the law. This is why concepts like marital rape, domestic violence and housework are problematic, not to say paradoxical, concepts for much political theory.
They are problematic because, in the very act of referring to them,
we imply that they both are and are not legitimate objects of legal
or political concern. In so far as something is work, it is public and
requires the payment of a wage, but in so far as it is *house*work it is
a private matter, and does not require the payment of a wage. Again,
in so far as something is violence, it is a criminal act, but in so far
as it is *domestic* violence it is a private matter, which is not the law's
business.

This distinction between public and private sprang in part from
the contention that women and men have different natures. But it
survives the apparent death of that belief, and sustains a problematic relationship between women and the political world. It sustains
a mode of thinking in which much of the work which women do as
wives and mothers falls outside political and legal consideration and
thus renders women (especially wives) largely invisible politically. In
insisting on women's 'special' qualities, Mary Wollstonecraft is
raising the question of why women's work in the home is deemed
irrelevant to politics: she is challenging the distinction between
public and private, home and state on which modern political
thought is premised, and she is asking why political philosophers see
the home as the place where politics ends, rather than as the place
where it should, and indeed does, begin.

The issues here are complex, and persist into late twentieth-century
feminist theory. If some of us feel the inequity of a world in which

women's work – housework – does not attract social and political recognition in the form of a wage, others of us will ask what there is to be said for a world in which everything is done for a wage, or is not done at all, and we will suspect that this is, ultimately, a world in which we know the price of everything and the value of nothing. I have made no attempt to solve this problem, but only to note that it was a problem which Mary Wollstonecraft saw clearly and whose root lies not in any inconsistency between her life and thought, but in the dilemmas generated by political philosophers who came before her, and sustained by political philosophers who have come after her.[22]

2
John Stuart Mill and Harriet Taylor on Women and Marriage

This paper focuses on two works of nineteenth-century feminism: Harriet Taylor's essay *The Enfranchisement of Women*, and John Stuart Mill's *The Subjection of Women*.[1] My aim is to indicate that these texts are more radical than is usually believed: far from being merely criticisms of the legal disabilities suffered by women in Victorian Britain, they are important moral texts, which anticipate central themes within twentieth-century radical feminism. In particular, *The Subjection of Women* is not merely a liberal defence of legal equality; it is a positive statement of the inadequacy of 'male' conceptions of reason and its powers. So understood, I shall argue, it coheres with Mill's other moral and political writings, and draws much of its persuasive power from the doctrines advanced in Harriet Taylor's *The Enfranchisement of Women*.

The structure of my argument is as follows: first, I shall contrast nineteenth-century commentary on *The Subjection of Women* with twentieth-century criticism of it. The aim here is to draw attention to the gulf which separates the two. Where nineteenth-century commentators interpreted Mill as presenting a radical (and shocking) moral text, twentieth-century commentators, including feminists, have construed him largely as an apologist for liberal political theory who emphasized the inequity of legal disadvantage but was unmindful of the social structures which sustained and fostered it.

Second, I shall suggest that Mill's nineteenth-century critics were more nearly right than their twentieth-century counterparts. His text is indeed both moral and radical, and its radicalism is, I shall claim, its most important facet, both for Mill himself and for us.

Finally, I shall indicate the ways in which Mill's relationship with Harriet Taylor (both intellectual and emotional) served to inform the doctrines of *The Subjection of Women*. Far from being simply a rational liberal, compromised by his emotional commitment to a more radical and socialist feminist, Mill was, in *The Subjection of Women*, advocating the rejection of the reason/emotion dichotomy itself. This rejection brings him closer to modern feminism, and at the same time casts doubt on the attempt to distinguish between those of his thoughts which were 'reasoned' and those which were claimed to be merely the result of keeping the company of Harriet Taylor. Where his contemporary critics argued that his relationship with her impaired his judgement, he himself was determined to show that the very idea of judgement as something inherently superior to emotion or intuition, was itself flawed. I begin, then, with the nineteenth-century reception of Mill's work.

A work of rank moral and social anarchy

The publication of *The Subjection of Women* in 1869 was timed to coincide with the growing parliamentary and political movement for the reform of the franchise and, especially, with the campaign for votes for women. Although Mill's biographer, St John Packe, alludes to some buffoonery in the lobbies when the question of female suffrage was raised in the House of Commons,[2] other commentators have noted the more general seriousness with which the issue was treated in Parliament, and Ann Robson concludes that 'through all those years the question of the removal of women's political disabilities was . . . hardly ever, treated as a laughing matter in the House of Commons'.[3]

By contrast, *The Subjection of Women* outraged Mill's contemporaries. St John Packe says, 'of anything Mill ever wrote, *The Subjection of Women* aroused the most antagonism. Those who were always hostile became more hostile still . . . and even his friends were horrified.'[4] Even at its worst, the Parliamentary campaign had caused only amusement, never outrage, but with *The Subjection of Women*, Mill had finally gone too far. Almost all the commentators of the time (both friend and foe) emphasize not the legal demands which Mill made on behalf of women, but rather the moral assumptions which underpin those demands. Predictably, James Fitzjames Stephen was

appalled and declared the work to be 'practically indecent' in its 'pro-
longed and minute discussions about the relations between men and
women'. 'I consider it unsound in every respect,' he said. 'I think it
rests upon an unsound view of history, an unsound view of morals,
and a grotesquely distorted view of facts.'[5] Significantly, it was not
the legal demands which Fitzjames Stephen took as his major target;
rather it was Mill's moral vision which outraged and appalled him.
And in this, he was not alone. Fredric Harrison declared the work to
be one of 'rank moral and social anarchy'; *Blackwood's Magazine* com-
mented on Mill's 'intense arrogance and incapacity to do justice to
the feelings or motives of all from whom he differs'; and even his
friend, Charles Kingsley, thought Mill imprudent in making public
pronouncements on matters which, says Kingsley, 'I have found it
wisest to keep to myself'.[6]

In brief, what was most objectionable about *The Subjection of
Women* was not its argument for women's suffrage (which in any case
occupies a comparatively small part of the text), nor its general call
for the improved legal status of women (which, as we have seen, had
gained considerable support in Parliament). What was most objectionable was Mill's view of the proper moral relation between the
sexes. Again, Fitzjames Stephen puts the matter plainly. He writes:
'No-one contends that a husband ought to have power to order his
wife about like a slave and beat her if she disobeys him. Such conduct
in the eye of the law would be cruelty and ground for separation,'
but Mill's 'tacit assumption that it is a degradation ever to give up
one's will to the will of another appears to me the root of all evil'.[7]

Thus, in its own day, *The Subjection of Women* was thought to be
'indecorous', 'arrogant', 'indecent', 'a work of moral anarchy' and
'the root of all evil'. By contrast, twentieth-century commentaries on
the text contain very few references to its moral argument, and it is
often interpreted as nothing more than a catalogue of the legal disabilities suffered by Victorian women, coupled with a series of plati-
tudes about their appropriate remedies. Since the legal injustices have
now been removed, the argument goes, Mill's text is of archaeo-
logical interest only. It is a quaint period piece which stands at a distance from his other moral and political writings and contains little
of interest in the late twentieth century.

Moreover, this general conclusion is not confined to the less
enlightened male commentators, but applies equally to many

feminist critics, who are often uneasily apologetic in their presenta-
tion of Mill's argument. Kate Soper, for example, argues that *The Subjection of Women* may be criticized 'for concentrating overmuch on
the removal of the legal forms of oppression and too little on the
material factors underlying the inequality of women before the law',
but she excuses Mill by noting that it would be wrong to make too
much of this criticism when 'at the time of his writing women were
legally little better off than bond slaves'.[8] Similarly, Julia Annas
claims that 'there is some truth in the accusation that Mill's thinking about sexual differences is shallow. He is not aware of the mas-
sive changes required in people's desires and outlooks before sexual
equality becomes a reality and its effects something people see as
beneficial.'[9] Finally, Carole Pateman draws an unfavourable comparison between Mill's views on marriage and those of William
Thompson. Thompson acknowledges that 'to bring the audacious
falsehood of the marriage contract to an end, not only sweeping
political and economic changes are required, but also radical change
in what it means to be a masculine or feminine sexual being'. Mill,
by contrast, 'explicitly equates a woman's choosing to marry with a
man's choice of career' and he assumes that if marriage were to
become a freely negotiated contract, women would still expect, and
choose, to provide domestic service.[10]

All these commentators, in their different ways, accuse Mill of
undue caution in his discussion of the subjection of women and all
complain that he took legal remedies to be sufficient for what were
really deep-rooted social ills. There is, however, a conspicuous silence
about the *moral* content of *The Subjection of Women* and, in particular, about the fact (as I believe it to be) that Mill's primary reason for
advocating legal change was that such change constituted the surest
route to moral improvement. It is this commitment to moral improvement which, I believe, dominated his thinking and outraged
his contemporary critics, but it is also this which has been neglected
since the nineteenth century.

The moral argument in Mill

What, then, are the grounds for advocating a moral rather than
a legal interpretation of *The Subjection of Women*? One answer is
provided by examining, not the catalogue of injustices suffered by

Victorian women, but rather the nature of the mischief which Mill believes these injustices exemplify. Of course, he thinks inequality to be wrong in itself, and to be a source of misery and unhappiness. He also believes that it diminishes the pool of talent available to the human race, and that it is therefore wasteful and profligate. But beyond all this, he believes that inequality is wrong *because it hinders moral progress and improvement.* Thus, at the beginning of the essay he advocates changes in the existing laws *on the grounds* that these are necessary for human improvement and the removal of those 'barbarisms' which men cling to in the face of progress and of moral and spiritual transition.[11] And similarly, at the end of the essay he declares that '*the moral regeneration* of mankind will only really commence when the most fundamental of social relations is placed under the rule of equal justice, and when human beings learn to cultivate their strongest sympathy with an equal in rights and in cultivation'.[12] For Mill, the moral health of society is the highest good, calling for constant care and sustenance if decay is not to set in. As Stefan Collini has put it: 'Mill is a moral coach, keeping the national conscience in trim, shaming it out of flabbiness, urging it on to yet more strenuous efforts.'[13] It is this moral regeneration which is Mill's fundamental aim, and it is his specific conception of what such 'regeneration' might involve that so appalled his contemporaries.

I shall now attempt to substantiate this claim further – first by discussing the connections between John Stuart Mill's *The Subjection of Women* and Harriet Taylor's *The Enfranchisement of Women*, and then by indicating what I take to be the precise nature of moral improvement as far as the woman question is concerned. Additionally, I shall indicate the ways in which *The Subjection of Women* draws upon arguments already advanced by Harriet Taylor and anticipates some of the doctrines of modern radical feminism.

The Subjection of Women and *The Enfranchisement of Women*

There is, in modern commentary on the two essays (*The Subjection of Women* and *The Enfranchisement of Women*), a degree of intellectual schizophrenia to which I wish to draw attention. Many of Mill's contemporaries, appalled by the arguments adduced in *The Subjection of Women*, interpreted them as a temporary aberration attributable to the unwholesome influence of Harriet Taylor and at odds with Mill's other philosophical writings. Nor has the tendency altogether disappeared in more recent commentary. Diana Trilling declares Taylor to be 'one of the meanest and dullest ladies in literary history, a monument of nasty self-regard, full of injured vanity, petty egoism, and ambition'.[14] Similarly, Phyllis Rose deems Harriet Taylor to be a woman 'of strong and uncomplicated will who dominated a guilt-ridden man,'[15] and Gertrude Himmelfarb has blamed Mrs Taylor for all the intemperate excesses of Mill's philosophy, including his commitment to feminism.[16] As Carole Pateman scathingly remarks, 'philosophers must clearly choose their wives with care or woman's natural political subversion will undermine the work of the mind.'[17]

Moreover, and however uncharitable these views may be, they are factually, if not evaluatively, consistent with Mill's own view of the situation, which was that the essays on the woman question were a seamless web – the joint product of himself and his wife – and that he had been immeasurably influenced by her in his work. Whether that influence was for good or ill is, of course, a separate question. By contrast, the friends of Mrs Taylor tend to highlight the differences between the two texts, in particular the greater radicalism of *The Enfranchisement of Women*, and they use that evidence to support the claim that Mrs Taylor was indeed sole author of the work and that it was not, as is sometimes claimed, the work of John Stuart Mill. How, then, can they square their judgement with the persistent claims made by Mill that he and she were as one?

Again, the answer does not lie in concentrating on the catalogue of ills which afflicted Victorian women (for here there certainly are significant differences between the two texts), but rather on the mischief of which those ills were merely a symptom. I have suggested already that Mill's main aspiration is for the moral improvement of mankind. It is this which he believes to be the most important reason for resolving the woman question, and it is this which so outraged his contemporary critics. But this is also one of the main themes of Harriet Taylor's earlier essay, *The Enfranchisement of Women*. Taylor makes repeated reference to 'the progress of improvement', and to the need for 'improvement in the moral sentiments of mankind', 'the rejection of all that is coarse and low', the 'elevation of character and intellect' and 'mental companionship which is improving'. Echoing Mill, as Collini interprets him, she writes:

a mind which learns to be satisfied with what it already is – which does not incessantly look forward to a degree of improvement not yet reached – becomes relaxed, self-indulgent, and loses the spring and tension which maintain it even at the point already attained ... for the interest, therefore, not only of women but of men, and of human improvement in the widest sense, the emancipation of women, which the modern world often boasts of having effected ... cannot stop where it is.[19]

Again, the mischief which is inherent in inequality is that it constitutes a barrier to moral improvement, and it is moral improvement which most exercises both John Stuart Mill and Harriet Taylor.

Further evidence for this thesis is found in the early essays on marriage and divorce. Taylor's short essay concentrates almost entirely on the necessity of progressing from a semi-civilized to a civilized state, and predicts that marriage laws, of whatever complexion, will be irrelevant 'when the whole community is really educated'.[20] Similarly, Mill takes marriage laws as being evidence of sensuality and lack of civilization. 'Popular morality would never,' he says, 'in a civilized or refined people have imposed any restraint upon freedom.'[21]

Again and again in these texts we find indications that John Stuart Mill and Harriet Taylor are urging, not legal improvement only, but a complete revision of the *moral* relationship between the sexes. Their advocacy of legal alteration is subordinate to this and motivated by it. Perhaps the clearest evidence is to be found in Mill's early essay on marriage, where he denounces the then marriage laws as 'made by sensualists, for sensualists, to bind sensualists', and goes on to urge that the framers of the law are ignorant of the care of the soul, of 'higher degrees of happiness', and of 'civilisation and refinement'.[22] In brief, the tone of all the essays on the woman question (*The Subjection of Women*, *The Enfranchisement of Women*, and the early essays on marriage and divorce) is informed by the high moral purpose which they are meant to serve.

But if Mill's nineteenth-century critics were more nearly right than their twentieth-century counterparts, and if it is indeed the case that Mill's writings on the woman question are underpinned by a concern, shared with Harriet Taylor, for the moral improvement of mankind, then what would such improvement consist in? I shall now elaborate on the understanding of moral improvement implicit in both Mill and Taylor, and draw some comparisons between their doctrines and the tenets of some modern radical feminism. My aim here is to suggest that twentieth-century feminist critics of Mill have been more apologetic than they need be about his feminism. When understood as a plea for moral and spiritual improvement, Mill's writings on the woman question may be seen to anticipate some important conclusions of radical feminism. Moreover, given his close relationship with Harriet Taylor, this conclusion should not surprise us.

Moral improvement and radical feminism

It is important to note at the outset that there is no single Bible of radical feminism. Rather, it has grown, changed and developed over the years, and different writers take different themes as central. However, my purpose is not to provide an exhaustive specification of radical feminism, but simply to pick out some themes character-istic of it, and to indicate the ways in which these themes are present (albeit in embryonic form) in *The Subjection of Women*, *The Enfran-chisement of Women*, and the early essays on marriage and divorce. Specifically, there are two themes which I wish to explore here: the first is radical feminism's understanding of sexuality and of the rela-tionship between men and women; the second is the reason/emotion dichotomy. In each case, I shall examine a central thesis of radical feminism and compare it with the themes of the Mill–Taylor writ-ings on women and marriage.

Sexuality and sensuality

In the area of sexuality, radical feminism is characterized in part by its emphasis on woman as sexual slave, and on the coerciveness of marriage in patriarchal societies. Women are forced into marriage, not by laws merely, but by the very structure of society itself. More-over, this societal pressure demands that women become, not simply slaves, but *willing* slaves. Alison Jaggar sees this appeal to the coercive nature of society, distinct from its laws, as *the* root difference between liberal feminism and radical feminism. She writes:

> In response to the stigmas of patriarchal ideology, liberal feminism has sought to rehabilitate the reputation of prostitutes by asserting that prostitution is a legitimate job option for women, provided that no coercion is involved. The liberal conception of coercion is, however, much narrower than radical feminist conceptions . . . Radical feminists point out the total coerciveness of the social system in which the primary criterion for evaluating women, other than their fertility, is their sexual attractiveness to men. For this reason, radical feminists assert that even marriage, under patriarchy, is a form of prostitution or sexual slavery.[23]

And so it is for Mill and Taylor. Their texts abound with comments on the social coercion of women who 'choose' marriage, and in particular on the educational conditioning and social expectations which guarantee that women will 'opt' to become wives and mothers. Thus, Harriet Taylor's early essay laments that 'women are educated for one single object – to gain their living by marrying', and she goes on to claim that 'when the whole community is really educated, though the present laws of marriage were to continue, they would be perfectly disregarded, because no-one would marry'.[24] Again, the real mischief which she identifies is not the liberal mischief of inequality under the law, but a more radical mischief, buried deep within the structure of society – the mischief which dictates that women have no real option but to marry and, moreover, are socialized into the expectation that their career will lie in economic and sexual dependence.

Similarly, Mill inveighs against the social expectations which guarantee that in marriage a man will get 'not a forced slave but a willing one'. 'All women,' he says, 'are brought up from the very earliest years in the belief that their ideal of character is the very opposite to that of men; not self-will and government by self-control, but submission, and yielding to the control of others.'[25] Anticipating central themes in radical feminism, Mill and Taylor point both to the roots of oppression as lying in the tyranny of social expectation, and also to the ways in which that tyranny dictates that subservience and compliance shall be moral virtues in women, but weaknesses in men.

If, as Alison Jaggar has claimed, radical feminism is at least partly characterized by its belief that women are sexual slaves, and its insistence that 'the personal is political', then we should note that these beliefs are shared by Mill and Taylor. Famously, Mill declared that there are now no legal slaves except the mistress of every house, and he further urges that this situation is not simply the consequence of legal disadvantage, but also, and more importantly, of societal attitude: the notion of inherent superiority, he says, arises early in the mind of the schoolboy, 'it grows with his growth and strengthens with his strength; it is inoculated by one schoolboy upon another' and culminates, finally, in a 'sultan-like' sense of superiority over women.[26] Against this background, it is difficult to concur with those who claim that Mill never moves beyond reformist doctrines to consider the radical social changes that many believe to be the condition of genuine female emancipation. For like radical feminists, Mill believed degradation and drudgery to be the realities masked by the ideology of motherhood, romance and equality. Like them, he believed that a change in consciousness was necessary for the liberation of women. Like them, he believed that inequality does not depend on the law, but on the general conditions of human society. Moreover, he shared these views with Harriet Taylor who, in the central section of *The Enfranchisement of Women*, emphasizes not the legal disadvantages suffered by women, but the extent to which women have become, by custom, inured to their situation: 'custom hardens human beings to any kind of degradation, by deadening the part of their nature which would resist it. And the case of women is, in this respect, even a peculiar one, for no other inferior caste that we have heard of have been taught to regard their degradation as an honour.' And again, 'abnegation of self, patience, resignation, and submission to power, unless when resistance is commanded by other interests than their own, have been stamped by general consent as pre-eminently the duties and graces required of women.'[27] Not only law, but custom, social mores and expectations are the targets for Mill and Taylor as much as for modern radical feminism.

Reason and emotion

The second parallel I wish to draw between radical feminism and the theses of Mill's and Taylor's writings concerns their treatment of the relationship between reason and emotion. Radical feminists, it has been said:

> glorify women for precisely the same reasons that men have scorned and sometimes feared them; in so doing they give special value to the psychological characteristics that have distinguished women and men. They are looking for ways of expressing their vision of wholeness, which will transcend the patriarchal dualisms of self and world; nature and spirit; reason and emotion.[28]

Radical feminists are 'proud of the female culture of emotion, intuition, love, personal relationships, as the most essential human characteristics'. In short, they reassert and revalue traditional 'female' characteristics.[29]

Ironically, it is in its discussion of woman's nature that Mill's text has been thought to be most suspect. His claim that women are 'nervous', excitable, given to over-hasty generalizations, not good at abstraction, are a regular source of embarrassment to modern feminists. But there is, I believe, a discernibly radical streak here, and one which is in sympathy with the concerns of modern feminism.

Mill's essay on Bentham was published shortly before his essay on the poet Coleridge, and Mill speaks of these as 'the two great seminal minds of England in their age'. His aim in the essays is to draw attention to the differences and similarities between the two: the ways in which they complement one another, and the ways in which, for instance, Coleridge may make good the defects in Bentham's philosophy, and vice versa. He remarks:

> For among the truths long recognised by Continental philosophers, but which very few Englishmen have arrived at, one is, the importance, in the present imperfect state of mental and social science, of antagonistic modes of thought: which it will one day be felt are as necessary to one another in speculation, as mutually checking powers are in a political constitution.[30]

This is Mill's complementarity thesis, and it has its origins in his early mental crisis. In his *Autobiography* he tells us that he was released from mental depression partly by reading the poems of Wordsworth, which appealed perfectly to his emotions and expressed 'not mere outward beauty, but states of feeling and of thought coloured by feeling, under the excitement of beauty'.[31] His emergence from the mental crisis brought with it a reluctance to place total faith in powers of analysis and intellect. He searched now for people – poets, writers, artists – who could compensate for the defects in his own character and early education by providing emotion and intuition to complement his own rationality. He turned first to Carlyle: 'the good his writings did was not as philosophy to instruct, but as poetry to animate', and he continues:

> I did not deem myself a competent judge of Carlyle. I felt that he was a poet, and that I was not; that he was a man of intuition, which I was not, and that as such he saw many things before me which I could only, when they were pointed out to me, hobble after and prove, but that it was highly probable he could see many things which were not visible to me even after they were pointed out. I never presumed to judge him with any definiteness until he was interpreted to me by one greatly superior to us both – who was more a poet than he, more a thinker than I – whose own mind and nature included his and infinitely more.[32]

Of course, the one greatly superior to them both was Harriet Taylor, and in speaking of her Mill again makes reference to complementarity. What was important about Harriet Taylor was that she could make good the defects in Mill's character in respect of emotion, intuition and feeling. She was a poet, where Mill was only a thinker. She had intuitive insight, where he had only rationality. She was imaginative, where he was a mere engine of logic. These qualities fitted her to lead him in the path of moral development, to educate and improve him. Just as Bentham had only one eye without the insights of Coleridge, so Mill had only one eye without the insights of Taylor.

In her paper 'Mill and the Subjection of Women', Julia Annas refers disparagingly to Mill's claim that women are (by nature) capable of intuitive perception of situations and can bring 'rapid and correct insight into present fact'. 'Here,' Annas says, 'is the oldest cliché in the book: women are intuitive while men reason. If any cliché has done most harm to the acceptance by men of women as intellectual equals, it is this, and it is distressing to see Mill come out with it. It is even more distressing to find him patronisingly recommending to any man working in a speculative subject the great value of an intuitive woman to keep him down to earth.'[33]

However, there is an irony in Annas' interpretation. For, far from being patronizing and clichéd, Mill's complementarity thesis anticipates radical feminist accounts of the inadequacy of 'male' conceptions of reason and its powers. Radical feminists are characterized by their insistence on glorifying women for precisely the same reasons men have scorned and sometimes feared them. In *The Dialectic of Sex* the radical feminist writer Shulamith Firestone concedes that women are indeed intuitive rather than rational, emotional rather than logical.[34] Yet, she insists, what is often wrong with science is precisely that it ignores emotions. She advocates 'emotional science' as a corrective to the over-valuing of technology and its powers, much as Mill praised the corrective influence of the poet in Carlyle, and subsequently in Harriet Taylor. In Mill's eyes, emotion and intuition, far from being qualities to be scorned, were highly prized. They were the necessary but unrecognized complements to intellect. Without them, society itself was one-eyed and capable of seeing only half the truth. *The Subjection of Women* is thus akin to radical feminism in its extended argument for the revaluing of female qualities.

In conclusion, *The Subjection of Women* is, I suggest, more complex, more moral and more radical than has normally been supposed. It is a text which emphasizes the importance of social as well as legal disadvantage, and which advocates the revaluing of emotion and intuition as important correctives to the 'male' values of reason, intellect and logic. In these respects it is a text which owes much to Harriet Taylor, not only because it shares with her essays a commitment to the need for changed attitudes, but also because, through her, Mill learned that there are values other than reason and logic. He learned, as Wordsworth put it:

> How little those formalities to which
> With overweening trust alone we give
> The name of Education have to do
> With real feeling and just sense.[35,36]

3
The Practical and the Pathological

It is commonly held that Kant's discussion of freedom and his attempt to reconcile freedom and necessity is a complete failure. Having argued in the early part of *The Critique of Pure Reason* that everything in the phenomenal realm is causally determined, he is then saddled with the problem of explaining how there can be free actions for which the agent may properly be held to be morally responsible. His answer to this puzzle is to insist that there *can* be genuine freedom, but that such freedom is reserved for the noumenal realm. However, since ordinary decisions and events occur in the phenomenal realm, it would appear that they must be determined by previous decisions and events within that series. And if that is the case, then the alleged freedom for which Kant makes room does no honest work, or at any rate not the sort of work he wanted it to do – namely, to explain how a man might properly be held responsible for the actions he performs. It would seem that Kant succeeds in justifying freedom 'if anywhere, then everywhere.'[1]

More trouble looms for accountability when, in the *Groundwork*, Kant actually equates freedom with abiding by the moral law, for it is a consequence of this equation that there can be no freely performed, morally wrong action. All morally wrong actions are unfree. Moreover, it is argued that even in the later writings, where Kant explicitly distinguishes between *Wille* and *Willkür* and thus attempts to explain exactly how a man may be thought to be accountable for the wrong actions he performs, the banishment of freedom to the noumenal realm destroys utterly our ordinary notion of moral responsibility. 'The freedom Kant postulates has to play certain roles

in the description of the human condition. These . . . require that
freedom be driven out of its noumenal isolation into the empirical
realm where it conflicts after all with determinism.'[2] The enterprise
of banishing freedom to the noumenal realm is partly explained by
reference to other aspects of Kant's moral philosophy. In particular,
the desire to separate moral responsibility from considerations of
natural advantage is seen as a driving force, encouraging Kant to
construe freedom as existing only in the noumenal realm. Thus
Bernard Williams argues: 'it is the thought that moral worth must be
separated from any natural advantage whatsoever which, consistently pursued by Kant, leads to the conclusion that the source of
moral thought and action must be located outside the empirically
conditioned self. Kant's work is, in this respect, a shattering failure,
and the transcendental psychology to which it leads is, where not
unintelligible, certainly false.'[3] The blame, then, for the abortive
attempt to reconcile freedom and necessity may be firmly placed at
the door of Kant's desire to separate morality from natural advantage. Williams again:

> As Kant remarks in a famous and moving passage, some find that
> the human gesture comes naturally, some do not. To make moral
> worth, the supreme value achievable by human beings, dependent
> on such features of character, psychologically determined as they
> are, would be to make the capacity for moral worth a species of
> natural advantage; and this is both logically incompatible with
> the notion of *the moral*, and also in some ultimate sense, hideously
> unfair.[4]

Now obviously the freedom/necessity dichotomy is not to be crudely
mapped onto the reason/inclination dichotomy. Part of the point of
the *Wille/Willkür* distinction is to indicate that freedom consists in
the ability to choose between the morally right course of action and
others. Hence Kant's claim that:

> Freedom in the practical sense is the will's (*Willkür*) independence
> of coercion through sensuous impulses. For a will is sensuous in
> so far as it is pathologically affected i.e. by sensuous motives;
> it is animal if it can be pathologically necessitated. The human
> will is certainly arbitrium sensitivum, not, however, brutum, but

liberum. For sensibility does not necessitate its action. There is in man a power of self-determination independently of any coercion through sensuous impulses.[5]

So it seems clear that in his mature writings Kant does not insist that acting from inclination is thereby acting unfreely in a sense which denies freedom of the will. If I choose to do evil, I freely decide to let my sensuous impulses have their way, but these sensuous impulses do not necessitate the will's action, and I may be free despite having motives other than those which a completely free and moral being has. This thought is borne out by Kant's discussion of evil in *Religion Within the Limits of Reason Alone*, where he says of an evil man that 'his actions by their uniformity of conduct exhibit a natural connexion. But the latter does not render the vicious quality of the will necessary, for this quality is the consequence of freely assumed evil and unchangeable principles. This fact makes it only the more objectionable and culpable.'[6] Now whether this can be made out in a way fully consistent with Kant's doctrine of freedom and his alleged banishment of freedom to the noumenal realm is not something I wish to discuss here. My only point is that in the mature writings it seems clear *both* that Kant wishes to separate moral worth from natural advantage *and* that he believes the evil man to be properly blameable for the evil he performs. If we allow that in acting from character in this way the agent acts freely, how is that to be reconciled with the Kantian desire to separate moral worth from natural advantage? Surely character is itself largely a matter of natural advantage? 'Some find the human gesture comes easily, some do not.' The criticisms of anti-Kantians in this area standardly rest upon two beliefs: the first is a belief about Kant's moral philosophy; the second is a belief about the proper scope of moral evaluation. They claim that, according to Kant, emotions, attitudes, character traits are all more or less matters of natural advantage and as such not proper objects of moral evaluation. Furthermore, they argue that Kant was wrong to insist on the impropriety of evaluating a man morally in respect of those features of his character over which he has no control. In other words, they insist both that there are certain features of my character over which I have no control and that it is quite proper to assess me morally in respect of those features.

My aim here will be to show, first, that Kant's account of emotional motivation is more sophisticated than his critics allow, and second, that in so far as Kant urges upon us the need to refrain from evaluating a man in respect of those qualities over which he has no control, he is right to do so. If this can be made out, then it will not be necessary for Kant to banish freedom to noumenal isolation, or, at any rate, not something necessitated by anything in the moral philosophy. I begin with an example taken from Peter Winch's Inaugural Lecture, 'Moral Integrity':

> Mrs Solness in Ibsen's *Master Builder* is someone who is obsessed with the Kantian idea of 'acting for the sake of duty'. She does not appear, though, as a paragon of moral purity, but rather as a paradigm of a certain sort of moral corruption. No doubt her constant appeal to duty is a defence against the dangerous and evil resentments she harbours within her. For all that, it is possible to think that the situation would have been a good deal less evil if she had occasionally forgotten her 'duty' and let herself go. At least this might have cleared the air and opened the way for some genuine human relationships between her and her fellow characters.[7]

This picture of Kant's good man (or woman) as cold, unfeeling, performing duty for duty's sake through, as it were, clenched teeth, is not uncommon amongst modern moral philosophers. Nowell-Smith compares the Kantian good man to the Oxford don who 'disliked Common Room life and whose presence caused himself and others acute distress. Yet he attended Common Room assiduously. 'He would,' says Nowell-Smith, 'have done better to stay at home.'[8]

The picture of the Kantian good man provided by Nowell-Smith and Winch meshes in most easily with the position Kant adopts in *Groundwork*. Mrs Solness and the Oxford don are presumably meant to represent the man of good will who has, however, little sympathy in his heart. Of him Kant says:

> If, (being in other respects an honest fellow) he were cold in temperament and indifferent to the sufferings of others perhaps because, being endowed with the special gift of patience and robust endurance in his own sufferings, he assumed the like in others, or even demanded it; if such a man (who would in truth

not be the worst product of nature) were not exactly fashioned by her to be a philanthropist, would he not still find in himself a source from which he might draw a worth far higher than any that a good-natured temperament can have? Assuredly he would. It is precisely in this that the worth of character begins to show – a moral worth, and beyond all comparison the highest – namely, that he does good, not from inclination but from duty.[9]

This description of the cold man seems to me to be rather less like Winch's account of Mrs Solness or Nowell-Smith's Oxford don than, say, Canon Jocelyn in F.M. Mayor's novel *The Rector's Daughter*.

As he spoke of his wife, he smiled. His smile was rare and it encouraged Mary to do what she had never done before, fling her arms round him. She cried 'Oh, what shall I do without her?' His smile disappeared, but he spoke kindly. 'Yes, yes I am sure you will miss her.' He did not return the embrace, but extricating himself gently, he said, 'I think I should advise you to go to bed. You can do no good by staying up,' and went back to his study.[10]

This, I suggest, is a more accurate picture of the man in whose heart nature has implanted little sympathy. He is not, indeed, the most lovable of men, but he is not either 'the worst product of nature'. Nor is he a paradigm of a certain sort of moral corruption. But if there is a difference between these two, can Kant explain what that difference is? In particular, can he show exactly why Mrs Solness is indeed a paradigm of a certain sort of moral corruption? I think so, and I take my cue from a passage in *Groundwork* immediately following that quoted above in which Kant first distinguishes between practical and pathological love – love from duty and love from inclination. Here he says:

It is doubtless in this sense that we should understand the passages from scripture in which we are commanded to love our neighbour and even our enemy. For love out of inclination cannot be commanded, but kindness done from duty – although no inclination impels us, and even though natural and unconquerable disinclination stands in our way – is practical, not pathological, love, residing in the will and not in propensions of feeling, in principles of action and not of melting compassion; and it is this practical love alone which can be an object of command.[11]

Now even in this and the earlier passage, which seem to provide the model for Mrs Solness as a paragon of virtue, there are hints that Kant does not in fact have anything like Mrs Solness in mind. In the first place, he speaks of the man in whose heart nature has implanted *little* sympathy – not none at all. Indeed, he later rejects the idea that a man might be totally devoid of sympathy. Moreover, even whilst allowing that we cannot be commanded to love from inclination, he still insists that *kindness* is our duty – not mere kind acts, but actual *kindness*. In fact, of course, it is hard to see how there could be kind acts in the absence of kindness. Some acts may appear kind to the casual observer, but where they are performed from scorn or contempt they are not kind at all, but scornful or contemptuous. So even in *Groundwork* there are suggestions as to what may be morally relevant differences between Canon Jocelyn and Mrs Solness. It must nevertheless be admitted that the main message of the section quoted is to insist that love out of inclination cannot be commanded, and this endorses the standard view of Kant's good man as cold and unfeeling. However in the later moral writings, Kant revises his position, stating that:

> the command to love our neighbour applies, within limits, both to love from obligation and to love from inclination. For if I love others from obligation, I acquire, in the course of time, a taste for it and my love, originally duty-born becomes an inclination.[12]

Now the claim that love from obligation will, in time, become love from inclination is not based on any high degree of optimism, but on the further claim that every man will, from the outset, have some degree of 'emotional love'. Thus, in *Metaphysics of Morals* Kant tells us that:

> there can be no duty to have a moral feeling, or to acquire it, for all consciousness of obligation presupposes this feeling in order that the constraint which lies in the concept of duty may be

known. Every man (as a moral being) has this feeling originally within himself. The obligation can extend only to cultivating it through wonder at its inscrutable origin.[13]

Now as Paton points out, the love spoken of here is not practical love, for practical love is a kind of goodwill:[14] it is our duty to do men kindnesses to the best of our ability. Nevertheless emotional and practical love are connected, the former being a precondition necessary for the concept of practical love as a duty. Moreover, we have a duty to cultivate emotional love in order that we may subsequently display it in acts of kindness. The situation then is this: it is undeniably true that we cannot love because we wish to love. Nevertheless, there is in all of us emotional love, for without this we could not recognize our duty at all, and we have a duty to cultivate this emotional love. The principle of practical love requires us to adopt an *attitude* of benevolence to all men. This attitude manifests itself in specific duties of love. Thus, in claiming that beneficence is a duty Kant incorporates the thought that this beneficence will be the manifestation of benevolence *as an attitude*. Hence the claim that 'beneficence is a duty and whoever often exercises this and sees his beneficent purpose succeed comes at last really to love him whom he has benefited'.[15]

In these passages we find evidence of what, for Kant, is the distinction between Mrs Solness and Canon Jocelyn. In the traditional picture, the Kantian good man is presented as completely devoid of moral feeling, but this cannot really be so. Kant tells us that 'no man is devoid of all moral feeling; for if he were totally unsusceptible to this sensation, he would be morally dead . . . his humanity would be dissolved into pure animality'.[16] (The fact is, of course, that Mrs Solness is not devoid of all feeling and never has been. Winch describes her as one who 'harbours' resentments. It is not simply that she has little or no sympathy in her heart. On the contrary, she has actually nurtured feelings of ill-will towards others, and although she cannot be blamed for the inclinations she has, she can be blamed for what she voluntarily does with them. She is thus, on Kant's account, and on any account, more culpable and objectionable than the man who has little feeling.)

In his book *The Passions* Robert Solomon extravagantly asserts that:

The myth of the Passions has so thoroughly indoctrinated us with its notion of passivity that we are no longer capable of seeing what we ourselves are doing. Once the myth is exploded, however, it is obvious that we make ourselves angry, make ourselves depressed, make ourselves fall in love.[17]

This is an exaggeration. It may be that there is little Mrs Solness can *now* do to alter her response to her fellow characters, but she is still morally culpable, for there is a strong sense in which she has brought herself to this pass by nurturing and endorsing her worse feelings, and by doing nothing to cultivate her better inclinations. As a consequence of this she cannot exhibit practical love at all, for practical love consists in doing kindnesses to one's fellow men. Canon Jocelyn's acts may be described as kindly: hers may not. They are patronizing, contemptuous, at the limit, scornful, and the more so because, as Kant points out, they are the consequence of 'freely assumed and unchangeable principles'.

However, even if Kant is able to show why Mrs Solness exemplifies a certain sort of moral corruption, his account will still differ radically from that of his opponents, who standardly favour abandoning duty in favour of the 'human gesture'. Thus Winch argues that the situation would have been better had Mrs Solness occasionally 'forgotten her duty and let herself go. This at least might have cleared the air and opened the way for some genuine human relationships between her and her fellow characters.[18] Two possibilities present themselves here: if it is really the case, as I have suggested, that Mrs Solness harbours resentment, then it is difficult to see how the situation could be *morally* better (or indeed better in any way) if she were to 'let herself go'. In situations such as this, appeal is sometimes made to honesty and openness, but I cannot see that this mysterious form of honesty would herald a moral improvement in the situation.

Alternatively, it might be thought that Mrs Solness does not harbour resentment, but is more like Canon Jocelyn, simply not well blessed with natural sympathy. In this case, the question of 'letting herself go' will not arise. There is nothing to let go of. Now it might be thought that this itself is a moral failing and Kant himself appears to concede that the situation is not ideal. He makes allowances for such men, encouraging us to remember that they may be, in other

respects, 'honest fellows', and insisting that 'coldness is not necessarily a thing to be condemned'. A cold man, where possessed of good
principles, will always be reliable, 'the coolness of the blood gives
order and regularity to our lives'.[19] It is important to remember that
Kant's targets here are the Romantics – those who, as Mary Midgley
puts it, glorify 'floods of tears, storms of passion, love at first sight,
scenes and embraces, spasms of self pity and finally, if possible,
shooting oneself in despair'.[20] It is against this background that he
urges us to remember the value of reliability and not to be too hard
on the man who is cold. Against this background, too, he denies the
value of a kind heart unaccompanied by kind deeds. 'If there is no
way I can help a man in suffering,' says Kant, I might as well turn
coldly away and say with the Stoics: 'it is no concern of mine. My
wishes cannot help him. We are kind hearted only in so far as we
actually contribute to the happiness of others: that alone betokens a
kind heart.'[21]

   This is a hard doctrine, for it is surely the case that a sympathetic
ear may often be of comfort. But in such a case I precisely *am* in a
position to alter the situation of the man who suffers. If I really can
do *nothing* to improve his predicament, it seems much less harsh to
suggest that I might do well to withdraw from the scene:

> I weep for you the Walrus said
> I deeply sympathise
> With sobs and tears he sorted out
> Those of the largest size
> Holding his pocket handkerchief
> Before his streaming eyes.[22]

I am not therefore persuaded that the value of the human gesture is
paramount here in the sense required by Kant's critics. Where the
individual harbours resentment, the human gesture is likely to be of
a sort which will make the situation conspicuously worse; where he
does not harbour resentment, but is simply cold and indifferent,
there will at least be reliability and regularity in his behaviour.
Bernard Williams asks: 'is it certain that one who receives good treatment from another more appreciates it, thinks the better of the giver,
if he knows it to be the application of principle, rather than the
product of emotional response? He may have needed, not the benefit

of universal law, but some human gesture.'[23] To which Kant may reply: 'is it certain that a man must prefer no good treatment at all to the ministrations of the reliably good man?' He, at least, will not refuse aid when it is needed. In his steady reliability there will be no hint of moral corruption. By contrast there surely is moral corruption in, for example, Bertrand Russell's declaration that while out on a bicycle ride one day he realized that he no longer loved his wife. His love for her, he says, 'evaporated' and he was no longer able to show any affection for her.[24] We think better of the human gesture only where it is coupled with steady goodwill, not where it may, without warning, flicker and disappear.

However, if all this is so, then Kant is able to show what is morally corrupt about Mrs Solness. Her corruption lies not directly and immediately in her current failure to have an inclination of love, but in her failure to cultivate that emotional love which everyone has as a necessary precondition of being able to recognize moral duty at all. Moreover, this duty to cultivate emotional love provides a sense in which we may, indirectly, be commanded to love, and that commandment will be more than an instruction to perform cold deeds. Against this background the standard objections to Kantianism (that it construes the emotions as wilful, capricious and randomly distributed, and that it ignores the value of the human gesture) are seen to rest upon an oversimplified account of Kant's moral philosophy. Since everyone has some capacity for emotional love, everyone may be expected or required to cultivate and nurture that capacity. In this way, the kind deeds performed will not be artificial, wooden or stilted. For sure, they will have been decided upon or chosen, but not in any morally objectionable sense. Quite the contrary, for what is morally objectionable, and indeed false, is the claim that one can do nothing about one's emotions. In general, we simply do not believe that individuals are unable to control their emotions, and this is precisely why, having 'let herself go', Mrs Solness should feel remorse and guilt.

Having said all that, there will, of course, be some cases in which I am unable to do anything about the emotion I feel. But these cases are far more rare than is usually thought and are barely countenanced by Kant, who insists that even those 'sentimental longings' he abhors are such that we might – and indeed must – 'seek to avoid them'.[25] Again, he is clearly thinking of a kind of unwholesome wallowing in self-pity, or pity for another of a sort which is at best ineffectual and at worst downright irritating.

In conclusion, then, the Kantian corpus, read as a whole, does not license behaviour akin to that of Mrs Solness, nor does Kant believe that all emotions are utterly outside our control. His emphasis on steady reliability and on the importance of rendering help where it is needed is an important response to the Romanticism of his day, and a response which ultimately the Romantics themselves recognized. In a letter to Chancellor von Müller in April 1818, Goethe extols Kant's 'immortal service' in bringing 'us all back from that effeminacy in which we were wallowing'.[26] We may all value the human gesture, but we should at the same time be wary of the Romantic who wears his heart on his sleeve, for such men change their shirts frequently.[27]

4
Time and Chance: Kantian Ethics and Feminist Philosophy

In the book of Ecclesiastes we read:

> And I returned and saw under the sun that the race is not to the swift, nor the battle to the strong, neither yet bread to the wise, nor yet riches to men of understanding, nor yet favour to men of skill; but time and chance happeneth to them all.[1]

'Time' and 'chance' have become the watchwords of much modern moral philosophy, with its emphasis on the centrality of tradition (Alasdair MacIntyre); the fragility of goodness (Martha Nussbaum); and the ubiquity of luck (Bernard Williams). Ecclesiastes conjectures what Richard Rorty confirms: that there is no escape from time and chance; no rationality independent of a tradition; no hiding place from the unfair judgements of an often hostile world.[2]

The ubiquity of time and chance serve, moreover, to emphasize the anti-Kantian tenor of much modern moral philosophy. MacIntyre's insistence on the contextual nature of rationality, his claims that rationality exists only within a tradition, and that progress in rationality is achieved only from a point of view, contrast with the Enlightenment enterprise of moving, by valid argument, from premises about a decontextualized human nature to conclusions about the authority of timeless moral rules. Similarly, Nussbaum's assertion of the fragility of goodness (the impossibility of guaranteeing immunity from the adversity of a contingent world), contrasts with the Kantian claim that morality is supreme and invulnerable to luck. And Rorty's advice that we try not to want anything beyond history and institutions contrasts with the Kantian insistence on a core, rational self which transcends history and socialization.[3] Moreover, such demands for a recognition of the contingency of life fit well with feminist calls for a rejection of Kantian *method*, as well as Kantian conclusions: for a mode of thinking which is contextual and narrative rather than abstract and universal, and for increased attention to the detail and particularity of individual cases, rather than the imposition of abstract moral rules.[4]

In brief, the Kantian enterprise, as traditionally understood, employs premises in order to reach conclusions about universality, rationality and necessity; the anti-Kantian backlash invokes narrative in order to adduce considerations about context, emotion and contingency. Where Kantianism searches for the common element of rationality which lies beneath the layers of socialization, the anti-Kantian sees such socialization as going 'all the way down' – as being itself the bedrock which defines what we are. There is no core self which underpins the vagaries of the fickle world; there is only the fickle world, which acts upon and constitutes us.

Perhaps the most graphic (though not the most subtle) way in which to display the relevant differences between Kantians and anti-Kantians is by appeal to two literary texts: the first is a poem by the ancient Greek writer, Pindar; the second a section from Shelley's epic poem, *Prometheus Unbound*. Pindar writes:

> But human excellence
> Grows like a vine tree
> fed by the green dew
> raised up, among wise men and just,
> to the liquid sky.
> We have all kinds of needs for those we love –
> Most of all in hardships, but joy, too,
> Strains to track down eyes that it can trust.[5]

The emphasis here is on human beings as vulnerable and needy creatures whose well-being is determined by things outside their control. In order to flourish, the vine requires sunshine and rain, the green dew and the liquid sky. It has, however, no power over the availability of these things, nor can it control the circumstances which determine its ability to flourish. And we, in turn, are like the vine.

We too are vulnerable, needy, dependent creatures whose flourishing is a matter of chance and circumstance. We cannot dictate how life will go for us, nor can we guarantee that the world will provide the things we need in order to flourish. Human beings, like things in nature, are all victims of time and chance.

However, this view of human nature contrasts starkly with that provided by Shelley, who writes, in *Prometheus Unbound*:

> The loathsome mask has fallen, the man remains
> Sceptreless, free, uncircumscribed, but man
> Equal, unclassed, tribeless and nationless,
> Exempt from awe, worship, degree, the king
> Over himself; just, gentle, wise: but man
> Passionless? – no, yet free from guilt or pain,
> Which were, for his will made or suffered them,
> Nor yet exempt, though ruling them like slaves,
> From chance and death and mutability.[6]

By contrast with Pindar, Shelley presents a picture of human beings as controlling time and chance. Man, for him, is a ruler – sceptreless and free – an agent, not a victim, the actor, not the acted upon. Shelley presents us with a vision of post-Enlightenment, Kantian man as one who controls, who dominates the outside world by virtue of his power of reason and of choice; whereas Pindar presents us with a vision of man as a victim, determined by the contingencies of life and unable to control his own destiny. For Pindar, man is a powerless creature, sunk in a world not of his own making; for Shelley, man is essentially a chooser, able to influence and partly control, if not conquer, the vagaries of time and chance.

Feminists and anti-Kantians have united in subscribing to something like Pindar's picture of the human predicament, whereas Kantians are more usually characterized by their affinity with (something like) Shelley's account. Kantian optimism rests on the belief that, in the moral realm at least, we may gain immunity from the contingencies of life; anti-Kantian and feminist pessimism is founded on the belief that time and chance happen to us all: that like the vine we cannot always, or with any degree of certainty, determine the way life will go for us.

My aims in this chapter are three-fold: first, to express some doubts about the alleged congruence between feminist moral theory and the arguments of the anti-Kantians referred to earlier (more specifically, to express doubts about the alleged similarity between feminists like Carol Gilligan, Virginia Held and Sara Ruddick on the one hand, and anti-Kantians such as Richard Rorty, Alasdair MacIntyre and Bernard Williams on the other). Second, and connectedly, to draw attention to different ways in which the doctrine of time and chance may be interpreted; and finally, to urge, in the light of these considerations, that feminists ought to pay more attention to central Kantian themes and distance themselves from at least some of the claims made by feminists and anti-Kantians. More specifically, I shall argue that feminist recognition that life is characterized by its contingency must be distinguished from the related but distinct belief that we are all unutterably different one from another – that the contingencies which determine our lives are also chasms which separate us. In particular, the claim that life is characterized by its contingency must be distinguished from the claim that the contingencies of women's lives are also chasms which separate them from men. For ultimately, I shall suggest, the failure to make this distinction will separate women from women, and will jeopardize feminism itself. For this reason, we must take care to understand the different ways in which it may be true that time and chance happen to us all. I begin, therefore, with a brief discussion of some of the main tenets of feminist moral theory of the Gilligan–Held–Ruddick variety.

Feminism and birthright

In her article 'Liberty and Equality from a Feminist Perspective', Virginia Held refers to those (like Kant) who argue for equality 'on the basis of an abstract moral principle rather than an empirical description'. And she criticizes their stance claiming that:

> their justifications of such a principle often rest on the observations that we are not all so different: we are all born, feel pain, and die. And as moral and political arguments are extended to women it may be supposed that such characterisations apply equally to women. But let us pause. From the point of view of those who give birth, all this changes. We give birth, and you do

not. This is a radical difference, and the fact that you lack this capacity may distort your whole view of the social world . . . occasionally, for those who give birth, equality will be an important concept, as we strive to treat children fairly and have them treat each other with respect. But it is normally greatly overshadowed by such other concerns as that the relationship between ourselves and our children and each other be trusting and considerate.[7]

Held's argument inverts traditional (or at least stereotypical) Kantian argument in three distinct ways: first, she draws attention to the differences which divide rather than the similarities which unite human beings. Second, she employs those differences to argue for the priority of trust and consideration over liberty and equality. Finally, and connectedly, she gives priority to particular relationships over abstract principles.

So where Kantianism searches for the core self which is common to all (a self which specifies our essential similarity and rational beings), Held discovers the 'radical differences' which are neglected or disguised by Kantian moral theory. Where Kantianism sees this similarity as justifying the priority of equality and liberty, Held sees equality and liberty as secondary to consideration and trust. Where Kantianism concerns itself with the application of abstract rules of justice, Held favours the context and narrative of specific human relationships as the basis for interpreting what a particular situation calls for. In very general terms Held, in common with other prominent feminists, denounces the search for a core self as one which has neglected the differences which divide us, and which has issued only in the discovery of the male self. Ultimately, she concludes, there can be no morality of humanity unless adequate attention is paid to experience – in particular, to the experience of women and the practice of mothering.

There are certainly striking similarities between this sort of approach to moral philosophy and the approach favoured by the anti-Kantians referred to earlier. Held's emphasis on context and narrative echoes Rorty's desire for a liberal utopia in which there will be a general turn away from theory and towards narrative. Her emphasis on trust and consideration reflects the move away from an ethic of justice and towards an ethic of care, and her insistence on the 'radical difference' between women and men reinforces the denial that there is a single self to be discovered once socialization has been peeled away.

However, beneath the superficial similarities there lurk important differences between this kind of feminist argument and the anti-foundationalism of, for example, Richard Rorty. Specifically, where Rorty sees the differences between individuals as being one of the most serious problems thrown up by the rejection of Kant's doctrine of the rational self, Held sees it as providing the motivation for a rejection of Kantianism. For Rorty, the denial of a core, rational self leaves a problem in its wake – the problem of enabling people to see others as similar to themselves, and thus of providing them with a reason to act for the common good – a motivation to solidarity, as he calls it. For Held, however, the denial of a rational self simply confirms the suspicion that there is no such common good, no set of reasons which will commend themselves to all.

The denial of a rational self may therefore take us in one of two directions: robbed of the obvious explanation of solidarity (of the motivation to a common good), we may either (with Rorty) search for an unobvious explanation, or we may conclude (with Held) that solidarity is a chimera. Feminists and anti-Kantians, though united in their rejection of a self which triumphs over contingency, are divided in the paths they follow once they have rejected it. But it makes a difference which path we take. To deny that we may escape from the contingency of life is but a short step from asserting that we are radically different one from another – so different that the prospects for solidarity are depressingly bleak. For this reason, feminists need to be clear about the differences between different forms of anti-Kantianism and, in particular, about the precise reasons they have for rejecting Kant's search for an escape from the vagaries of time and chance.

Time, chance and solidarity

Given these differences both within and between feminists and anti-Kantians, it is important to say something about the purpose which Kant's moral theory is meant to serve. By this I mean the deep motivation which lies behind the enterprise, rather than the virtues or defects of particular doctrines. Before rejecting the claim that, as moral agents, we are immune to the vagaries of time and chance, we should first inspect the reasons which motivate that thought. One of Kant's main aims in *Groundwork* is to provide, for ordinary individuals, solace in a world which is conspicuously unfair. Thus, Judith Shklar notes that:

> Anyone can in principle aspire to become a Kantian good character. It requires no special gifts of intelligence, beauty, wealth, or good luck. You do not have to be an aristocratic, superbly endowed Greek male to be a decent character. This is a thoroughly democratic liberal character, built to preserve his own self-respect and that of others, neither demanding nor enduring servility.[8]

In similar vein, Rorty refers to Kant's enterprise as one which aims to make the world safe for

> unimaginative, decent, honest, dutiful people . . . People with no special acuity of mind or intellectual curiosity . . . who, unlike the Christian saint, are not aflame to sacrifice themselves for love of the crucified Jesus.[9]

By extolling duty, and giving supreme importance to the good will, Kant renders such people paradigmatic moral agents, who may act impeccably despite (or perhaps even because of) their very ordinariness. To justify the belief that moral goodness is available even to the ordinary is therefore part of the motivation which governs *Groundwork*. It is the hope of moral immunity from time and chance which informs the Kantian enterprise, and it is the existence of a rational self which promises to provide that immunity. So Kant's moral theory recognizes the differences between people, but aims to provide consolation that those differences do not render moral goodness unattainable.

However, if it is the hope of an escape from time and chance which informs Kant's enterprise, it is the belief that there is no such escape which largely informs the theories of the anti-Kantians referred to earlier. Bernard Williams notes that 'most advantages and admired characteristics are distributed in ways which, if not unjust are at any rate not just, and some people are simply luckier that others'. Similarly Martha Nussbaum emphasizes the recalcitrance of the world to our good willing. There are, she says, some circumstances in which contingent commitments collide, and no amount of good willing can prevent them doing so. In both cases, the conclusion is the pessimistic one that even the decent character will sometimes be rendered impotent in the face of a hostile external world.

This is a laudably feminist conclusion, for the belief (poetically expressed by Pindar, and given philosophical expression by anti-Kantians) that we are beleaguered creatures, sunk in the realities of a cruel and hostile world, is a belief which reflects the facts of many women's lives. It is a contingent, but important fact that the model of man as Prometheus Unbound, controlling, sceptreless and free, is what it says it is – a model of *man* and not, or not recognizably, a model of woman. To the extent that this is so, the anti-Kantians are right to reject the core self and emphasize the fact that time and chance do indeed happen to us all.

None the less, a further, and less readily recognized, consequence may also follow from the rejection of the core self. For the Kantian rational self aims not only to immunize us against the vagaries of time and chance (the 'accidents of a step-motherly nature' and the 'recalcitrance of the contingent world'), but also to provide a unify-ing feature of human beings – a feature whose presence binds us together in a common humanity. If we reject the core self as a form of immunization against contingency, we reject also one of the most obvious explanations of common humanity. It follows that if there is to be solidarity between individuals, then that solidarity must be created, since (*ex hypothesi*) it cannot be discovered. Hence Rorty's ambition to create a utopia in which:

> Human solidarity would be seen not as a fact to be recognised by clearing away prejudice, or burrowing down to previously hidden depths, but, rather, as a goal to be achieved. It is to be achieved not by inquiry but by imagination, by the imaginative ability to see strange people as fellow sufferers, solidarity is not discovered by reflection, but created. It is created by increasing our sensitiv-ity to the particular details of the pain and humiliation of other, unfamiliar sorts of people.[10]

It is worth noting the gulf which separates this account from the account offered by Held. Where Rorty urges that we employ imagination in order to create similarities between people who are very different, Held urges that we simply acknowledge the radical differences between people of different gender. In other words, for Rorty, the recognition of difference is a problem which stands in need of a solution. For Held, the recognition of difference is simply a fact which has for too long gone unremarked by moral philosophers.

Held's position has two consequences for our understanding of morality: first, it reinforces the belief that time and chance are ubiquitous, in the sense that they define what we are (we are indeed creatures of circumstance, locked in a world we do not control). Second, and more importantly for my purposes, it reinforces pessimism about the possibility of encouraging solidarity between people. For the hope of solidarity is the hope that different people may come to see their similarities as more important than their differences. And this hope is crucial for morality generally, and for feminist morality in particular.

To propose an escape from time and chance can either be to propose that individuals may, in virtue of their rationality, escape from the contingency of moral life, or to propose that similarities between people (whether created or discovered) may provide a motivation to solidarity. It may be either an attempt to deny that time and chance can happen to us all, or an attempt to accept that time and chance can happen to us all, but to couple that acceptance with a denial that time and chance constitute us all. Where the existence of similarities is denied, then as individuals we become rooted in the contingencies of our own lives and, simultaneously, distanced from others who could be the objects of our good will. The thirst for a core self is thus a thirst both for personal immunity from time and chance, and a thirst for a more general justification of morality. By urging that there is no core self, no rational component which is common to us all, anti-Kantians simultaneously deny the invulnerability of morality to luck, and render problematic the motivation to morality.

In order to see why this is so, we should note that, in emphasizing difference, Held is not primarily concerned to emphasize the diferences between individuals. Rather, her concern is with the differences which separate groups of people, and in particular the differences which divide women (as child-bearers) from men. However, in emphasizing these differences, she largely ignores the fact that in

modern societies most people belong to several different and potentially conflicting groups: being a mother is only one facet of identity
(albeit a very important one) and for most women there are other
memberships and other demands not all of which are consonant
with the demands of being a mother.

By ignoring these different memberships, Held's view threatens to
become just as static and restrictive as the Kantian core self it was
intended to replace. For if her claim is simply that the experience of
being a mother is one which may contribute to and inform moral
theory, then the claim is in large part unobjectionable, but also, I
think, fairly uninteresting. In order to acquire interest, it has to
emphasize (as Held does) the *radical* nature of the difference between
those who have this experience and those who do not. It must urge
the priority of this experience over all others, and it must imply that,
at root, it is this experience which defines who one is and what one
is required to do. This, however, is a dangerous strategy, for at root
it presupposes an account of individual identity which is just as simplistic as the Kantian doctrine to which it is so firmly opposed. Beginning with the acknowledgement of contingent difference, it ends
with the assertion of unalterable similarity. A similarity, moreover,
which ultimately denies the possibility of solidarity between different people. So where the Kantian project aimed to explain the possibility of solidarity in the face of individual difference, this form of
feminism denies the possibility of solidarity precisely because of individual difference.

This denial should worry feminists, and is of special significance
to feminists (like myself) who are of a socialist persuasion: socialism
is characterized (at least partly) by the importance it vests in the
concept of solidarity, but if feminist moral theory is presented in such
a way as to make the motivation to solidarity problematic, then
socialist feminism is threatened. In her article 'Fraternity', Anne
Phillips writes:

> we should not act as if the only solidarity worth its name is the
> one that unites through every aspect of our existence. Rather, we
> should think of socialist unity as a complicated – maybe even
> painful – construction from many different solidarities, some of
> which will inevitably be in conflict.[11]

This, I suggest, holds true both of socialism and of feminism: feminists too should not act as if the only solidarity worth its name is the one that unites through every aspect of women's existence. This is not because such solidarity is a chimera, but because, in certain circumstances, it is destructive of basic feminist ideals.

In the next section, I shall describe an example of a case in which problems of solidarity arise. I shall ask what Kantianism, anti-Kantianism and feminism (in its various forms) have to say about the example, and I shall suggest that the solution to the problem depends crucially on adopting some basic Kantian assumptions. I shall conclude that, as individuals, we are indeed the victims of time and chance, and that it is exactly that fact which should encourage us to remember some of the more basic tenets of Kant's moral philosophy. Even if time and chance happen to us all, time and chance do not constitute us all, and it is that distinction which provides the deep motivation for Kant's moral theory.

Sisterhood and solidarity

The controversy surrounding the publication of Salman Rushdie's *Satanic Verses* in 1988 was one which generated acute conflict within the British liberal establishment, and particularly within the feminist movement, where respect for culture and tradition vie uneasily with the recognition that for Muslim women, culture and tradition may have an unacceptable face. On 9 March 1989, Southall Black Sisters and Southall women's section of the Labour Party, (subsequently re-formed as a sub-section of Women Against Fundamentalism) issued a statement which declared:

> We will not be dictated to by fundamentalists. Our lives will not be defined by community leaders.We will take up our right to determine our own destinies, not limited by religion, culture or nationality.[12]

The Southall demand may be interpreted in one of two ways, each of which is pertinent to the earlier discussion. It may be interpreted as the utterance of the Kantian rational self, the self which transcends socialization and culture, and which is the guarantee of common humanity despite diversity of circumstance. It may, in other words, be interpreted as a plea for immunity from time and chance, a Promethean cry for the right to reign uncircumscribed, sceptreless and free. Alternatively, the demand may be interpreted not as a rejection, but rather as a confirmation of the often problematic nature of socialization. It may be read as a reminder that one individual can be a member of many different groups which make different demands, not all of which can simultaneously be satisfied. The Southall women are Muslims, whose identity is determined by their membership of the Muslim community. They are also women, whose identity is determined by their gender. They inhabit a western, pluralist society, and their identity is formed by that membership too. Time and chance do indeed happen to them all, but time and chance pull in different directions. The differences which separate them as women from men may conflict with the differences which separate them as Muslims from western liberals. Defending the forms of feminism discussed above, Cheshire Calhoun writes:

> Too much talk about our similarities as moral selves, and too little talk about our differences has it moral dangers . . . Unless moral theory shifts its priority to knowledgeable discussions of human differences – *particularly differences tied to gender, race, class and power* – lists and rank orderings of basic human interests and rights as well as the political deployment of those lists are likely to be sexist, racist and classist. (my emphasis)[13]

This is true, but it can become a somewhat cosy and simplistic truth: where Kantianism allegedly ignores the differences between different people, and particularly the differences between women's lives and men's lives, some forms of anti-Kantianism attempt to remedy the defect by emphasizing, not difference, but multiplicities of similarities – similarities which may be traced to group membership – to gender, race and class. This is a dangerous strategy for feminists: appeal to a Kantian core self hypostatizes a single unity beneath diversity, and that unity is the ground of solidarity. By contrast, appeal to gender, race and class hypostatizes different unities and, in so doing, draws attention to different, and sometimes incompatible, loyalties which are at odds with the search for solidarity.

Thus, in the case of the Southall women, the demands of Islam may be in conflict with the expectations of western liberal society. Yet both are factors which form and inform their lives. They may therefore find that they are forced to choose between being good feminists and being good Muslims. Far from avoiding the dangers of racism, sexism and classism, the methods of some anti-Kantians may exacerbate those problems by their failure to address the fact that there can be tensions between the different groups.

If, as feminists, our strategy is to emphasize the radical differences which divide women from men, then we must recognize that there may be equally radical differences which divide women from women. Therefore, feminist moral theory must not rest content with the mere statement of difference, much less with the insistence on *radical* difference. It must also provide itself with a means of promoting solidarity through difference.

Kantian abstraction from the differences which divide us may indeed lead to the idealization of a single and spurious rationality which, allegedly, we share. We are not all the same, and the pretence that we are has damaged and continues to damage the interests of women. Nevertheless, the fact that we are not all the same should not lead to the simple conclusion that difference goes 'all the way down', and that these differences can be explained by simple reference to group membership – to race, class and gender. For this too is an idealization, distinct in kind, but no less dangerous in implication: an idealization which runs the risk of substituting the tyranny of group membership for the tyranny of universal rationality.

Therefore, when feminists deny the doctrine of the rational self and insist (properly and correctly) that 'time and chance happeneth to us all', it is important to be clear about the consequences of that denial. To reject talk of a rational self is, I believe, proper and legitimate, but to substitute for it talk of a female self, a Muslim self, a working-class self or a liberal self, is to ignore the possibility of conflict between the selves, and to condone the separatism which may result. In a multicultural society, separatism is too often our problem, and for that very reason, it can hardly be our solution. We must therefore resist the temptation to remedy a single Kantian abstraction (the abstraction which results in the doctrine of the rational self) by recourse to multiplicities of abstractions (the liberal self, the female self, the Muslim self, and so on).

However, if the move from a single unity to multiplicities of unities is to be avoided, so too is the move from Kantian abstraction to the celebration of individual difference. Again, in the Kantian scheme of things, it is the fact of difference which drives the moral theory. It is not itself the moral theory. In *Lectures on Ethics* Kant writes of the rogue:

> He may be a most wicked wretch, but who knows what drove him to it? With his temperament, wickedness may be no greater than a trifling fault of my own. If I look into his heart I can find in him too a feeling for virtue, and therefore in him too humanity must be loved.[14]

Kant in fact recognizes that time and chance happen to us all, but this is not a reason for resting content with the assertion of radical difference. On the contrary, it is the most powerful single reason for drawing attention to similarities where they exist, and for creating them where they do not. Like socialism, sisterhood must *unite*, but it must unite not simply by asserting the existence of solidarity amongst all women, but also by recognizing the need for the construction of solidarities between different women. This task will be a long and painful one, and it can succeed only if we bear in mind that, despite our differences, we are still and all similar one to another. We are all born, feel pain and die. 'All go unto one place; all are of the dust, and all turn to dust again', as we also read in the book of Ecclesiastes.[15]

5
Marital Faithfulness

And so the two swore that at every time of their lives, until death took them, they would assuredly believe, feel and desire exactly as they had believed, felt and desired during the preceding weeks. What was as remarkable as the undertaking itself was the fact that nobody seemed at all surprised at what they swore.[1]

Cynicism about the propriety of the marriage promise has been widespread amongst philosophers and laymen alike for many years. Traditionally, the ground for suspicion has been the belief that the marriage promise is a promise about feelings where these are not directly under the control of the will. G.E. Moore gives expression to this view when he remarks that 'to love certain people, or to feel no anger against them, is a thing which it is quite impossible to attain directly by the will', and he concludes that therefore the commandment to love your neighbour as yourself cannot possibly be a statement of your duty; 'all that can possibly be true is that it would be your duty if you were able'.[2] Thus, as Mary Midgley has pointed out, Moore renders the commandment irrelevant to us, since it is not in our power to do what it enjoins.[3] Moore's sentiments would presumably be endorsed by Russell, who tells of how his love for his wife 'evaporated' during the course of a bicycle ride. He simply 'realized', he says, that he no longer loved her and was subsequently unable to show any affection for her.[4] This, then, is one familiar objection to the marriage promise: that it is a promise about feelings, where feelings are not directly under the control of the will.

A second objection to the marriage promise is that it involves a commitment which extends over too long a period: promising to do something next Wednesday is one thing, promising to do something fifty years hence is quite another, and it is thought to be improper either to give or to extract promises extending over such a long period of time. This second objection has found philosophical support in the writings of Derek Parfit. In 'Later Selves and Moral Principles' Parfit refers to those who believe that only short-term promises can carry moral weight and counts it a virtue of his theory of personal identity that it 'supports' or 'helps to explain' that belief.[5]

Here I shall not discuss Parfit's theory of personal identity as such, but only the plausibility of the consequent claim that short-term promises alone carry moral weight: for it is the supposed intuitive plausibility of the latter which Parfit appeals to in defence of his theory of personal identity. If, therefore, the belief that only short-term promises carry moral weight can be undermined, that will serve, indirectly, to undermine any theory of personal identity which supports it.

Claiming that long-term promises do not carry any moral weight seems to be another way of claiming that unconditional promises do not carry any moral weight. Such an unconditional promise is the promise made in marriage, for when I promise to love and to honour I do not mutter under my breath, 'So long as you never become a member of the Conservative Party', or 'Only if your principles do not change radically'. Parfit's suggestion seems to be that all promises (all promises which carry any moral weight, that is) are, and can be, made only on condition that there is no substantial change in the character either of promisor or promisee: if my husband's character changes radically, then I may think of the man before me not as my husband, but as some other person, some 'later self'. Similarly, it would seem that I cannot now promise to love another 'til death us do part', since that would be like promising that another person will do something (in circumstances in which my character changes dramatically over a period of time), and I cannot promise that another person will do something, but only that *I* will do something. Thus all promises must be conditional, and all promises must be short-term. For what it is worth, I am not the least tempted to think that only short-term promises carry any moral weight, and it is therefore a positive *disadvantage* for me that Parfit's theory has this consequence, but even if it were intuitively plausible to claim that short-term promises alone carry moral weight, there are better arguments than intuitive ones and I hope I can adduce some here.

The force of Parfit's argument is brought out by his 'Russian nobleman' example, described in 'Later Selves and Moral Principles':

> Imagine a Russian nobleman who, in several years will inherit vast estates. Because he has socialist ideals, he intends now to give the land to the peasants, but he knows that in time his ideals may fade. To guard against this possibility he does two things. He first signs a legal document, which will automatically give away the land and which can only be revoked with his wife's consent. He then says to his wife 'If I ever change my mind and ask you to revoke the document, promise me that you will not consent'. He might add 'I regard my ideals as essential to me. If I lose these ideals I want you to think that I cease to exist. I want you to think of your husband then, not as me, but only as his later self. Promise me that you would not do as he asks.[6]

Parfit now comments:

> This plea seems understandable and if his wife made this promise and he later asked her to revoke the document she might well regard herself as in no way released from her commitment. It might seem to her as if she had obligations to two different people. She might think that to do what her husband now asks would be to betray the young man whom she loved and married. And she might regard what her husband now says as unable to acquit her of disloyalty to this young man – to her husband's earlier self. [Suppose] the man's ideals fade and he asks his wife to revoke the document. Though she promised him to refuse, he now says that he releases her from this commitment ... we can suppose she shares our view of commitment. If so, she will only believe that her husband is unable to release her from the commitment if she thinks that it is in some sense not *he* to whom she is committed ... she may regard the young man's loss of ideals as involving replacement by a later self.[7]

Now, strictly speaking, and on Parfit's own account, the wife should not make such a promise: to do so would be like promising that another person will do something, since she has no guarantee that *she* will not change in character and ideals between now and the time of the inheritance. Further, there is a real question as to why anyone outside of a philosophical example should first draw up a document which can only be revoked with his wife's consent and then insist that his wife not consent whatever may happen. But we can let these points pass. What is important here, and what I wish to concentrate on, is the suggestion that my love for my husband is conditional upon his not changing in any substantial way: for this is what the example amounts to when stripped of its special story about later selves. (In his less extravagant moods Parfit himself allows that talk of later selves is, in any case, a mere *'façon de parler'.*[8])

The claim, then, is that all promises must be conditional upon there being no significant or fundamental change in the character of the promisee. If my husband's character and ideals change it is proper for me to look upon him as someone other than the person I loved and married. This view gains plausibility from reflection on the fact that people can, and often do, give up their commitments. There is, it will be said, such an institution as divorce, and people do sometimes avail themselves of it. But although I might give up my commitment to my husband, and give as my reason a change in his character and principles, this goes no way towards showing that only short-term promises carry any moral weight, for there is a vital distinction here: the distinction between, on the one hand, the person who promises to love and to honour, but who finds that, after a time, she has lost her commitment (perhaps because of changes in her husband's character) and, on the other hand, the person who promises to love and to honour only on condition that there be no such change in character. The former person may properly be said, under certain circumstances, to have given up a commitment; the latter person was never committed in the appropriate way at all.

The wife of the Russian nobleman, by allowing in advance that she will love her husband only so long as he doesn't change in any of the aforementioned ways, fails properly to commit herself to him: for now her attitude to him seems to be one of respect or admiration, not commitment at all. Now she *does* mutter under her breath, 'So long as you don't become a member of the Conservative Party'. But the marriage promise contains no such 'escape clause'. When Mrs

Micawber staunchly declares that she will never desert Mr Micawber, she means just that. There are no conditions, nor could there be any, for otherwise we would fail to distinguish between respect or admiration *for the principles* of another and the sort of unconditional commitment *to him* which the marriage vow involves. There are many people whose ideals and principles I respect, and that respect would disappear were the ideals and principles to disappear, but my commitment to my husband is distinct from mere respect or admiration in just this sense, that it is not conditional on there being no change in his ideals and principles. I am now prepared to admit that my respect for another person would disappear were he revealed to be a cheat and a liar. I am not now prepared to admit that my love for my husband, my commitment to him, would disappear were he revealed to be a cheat and a liar. Perhaps an analogy will be illuminating here: in his article 'Knowledge and Belief', Norman Malcolm distinguishes between a strong and a weak sense of 'know', and says:

> In an actual case of my using 'know' in a strong sense I cannot envisage a possibility that what I say should turn out to be not true. If I were speaking of another person's assertion about something I *could* think both that he is using 'know' in a strong sense and that none the less what he claims he knows to be so might turn out to be not so. But in my case I cannot have this conjunction of thoughts, and this is a logical, not a psychological fact. When I say that I know, using 'know' in the strong sense, it is unintelligible to me (although perhaps not to others) to suppose that anything could prove that it is not so and therefore that I do not know it.[9]

Such is the case with commitment of the sort involved in the marriage vow. I promise to love and to honour, and in so doing I do not now envisage anything happening such as would make me give up that commitment. But, it might be asked, how can I be clairvoyant? How can I recognize that there is such a thing as divorce and at the same time declare that nothing will result in my giving up my commitment? The explanation lies in the denial that my claim to know (in the strong sense) or commitment (here) has the status of a prediction. My commitment to another should not be construed as a prediction that I will never desert that other. Malcolm again: 'The

assertion describes my present attitude towards the statement . . .
it does not prophesy what my attitude would be if various things
happened.'[10]

But if my statement is not a prediction, then what is it? It is
perhaps more like a statement of intention, where my claims about
a man's intentions do not relate to his future actions in as simple a
way as do my predictions about his future actions. Thus, if I predict
that A will do x and A does not do x, then my prediction is simply
false. If, on the other hand, I claim that A intends to do x and he
does not do x, it is not necessarily the case that my statement was
false: for he may have had that intention and later withdrawn it.
Similarly with commitment: if I claim that A is unconditionally committed to B, that is not a prediction that A will never desert B, it is
a claim that there is in A a present intention to do something permanently, where that is distinct from A's having a permanent intention. Mrs Micawber's claim that she will never desert Mr Micawber,
if construed as a commitment to him, is to that extent different from
a prediction that she will never desert him, for her commitment need
not be thought never to have existed if she does desert him. An
unconditional commitment to another person today, a denial today
that anything could happen such as would result in desertion of Mr
Micawber, is not incompatible with that commitment being given
up at a later date.

In brief, then, what is wrong in Parfit's example is that the wife
now allows that her commitment will endure only so long as there
is no substantial change in character. She should not behave thus,
because her doing so indicates that she has only respect for her
husband or admiration for his principles, not a commitment to him.
She need not behave thus, as there can be such a thing as unconditional commitment, analogous to intention and distinct from prediction in the way described. All this points to the inherent oddity
of the 'trial marriage'. It is bizarre to respond to 'wilt thou love her,
comfort her, honour her and keep her?' with 'Well, I'll try'. Again,
the response 'I will' must be seen as the expression of an intention
to do something permanently, not a prediction that the speaker will
permanently have that intention.

A further problem with the Russian nobleman example and the
claim that only short-term promises carry any moral weight is this:

when the wife of the Russian nobleman allows in advance that her commitment to her husband may cease if his principles change in any substantial way, she implies that a list of his present principles and ideals will give an exhaustive explanation of her loving him. But this is not good enough. If I now claim to be committed to my husband I precisely cannot give an exhaustive account of the characteristics he possesses in virtue of which I have that commitment to him: if I could do so, there would be a real question as to why I am not prepared to show the same commitment to another person who shares those characteristics (his twin brother, for example). Does this then mean that nothing fully explains my love for another and that commitment of this sort is irrationally based? I think we need not go so far as to say that. Certainly, when asked to justify or explain my love I may point to certain qualities which the other person has, or which I believe him to have, but in the first place such an enumeration of qualities will not provide a complete account of why I love him, rather it will serve to explain, as it were, his 'lovableness'. It will make more intelligible my loving him, but will not itself amount to a complete and exhaustive explanation of my loving him. Further, it may well be that in giving my list of characteristics I cite some which the other person does not, in fact, have. If this is so, then the explanation may proceed in reverse order: the characteristics I cite will not explain or make intelligible my love, rather my love will explain my ascribing these characteristics. A case in point here is Dorothea's love for Casaubon, which is irrationally based in that Casaubon does not have the characteristics and qualities which Dorothea thinks him to have. Similarly, in the case of infatuation the lover's error lies in wrongly evaluating the qualities of the beloved. An example here is Shakespeare's Titania, who 'madly dotes' on the unfortunate Bottom who is trapped in an ass's head. Titania addresses him thus:

> Come sit thee down upon this flowery bed
> While I thy amiable cheeks do coy
> And stick musk roses in thy sleek, smooth head
> And kiss thy fair, large ears my gentle joy.

And again:

> I pray thee, gentle mortal, sing again.
> Mine ear is much enamoured of thy note;
> So is mine eye enthralled to thy shape,
> And thy fair virtue's force perforce doth move me
> On the first view, to say, to swear, I love thee.[11]

Both cases involve some error on the part of the lover. In one case the error is a false belief about the qualities the beloved possesses; in the other it is an error about the evaluation of the qualities the beloved possesses. These two combine to show that there can be such a thing as a 'proper object' of love, and this will be the case where there is neither false belief nor faulty evaluation. The cases do not, however, show that in ascribing qualities and characteristics to the beloved the lover exhaustively explains and accounts for his love. The distinction between 'proper' love and irrationally based love, or between 'proper' love and infatuation, is to be drawn in terms of the correctness of beliefs and belief-based evaluations. By contrast, the distinction between love, on the one hand, and respect or admiration, on the other, is to be drawn in terms of the explanatory power of the beliefs involved. In the case of respect or admiration the explanatory power of belief will be much greater than it is in the case of love. For this reason my respect for John's command of modal logic will disappear, and I am now prepared to admit that it will disappear should I discover that he in fact knows nothing about modal logic. By contrast I am not now prepared to admit that my commitment to and love for my husband will disappear if I discover that my beliefs about his qualities and characteristics are similarly ill-grounded. W. Newton-Smith makes something like this point in his article 'A Conceptual Investigation of Love':

> Concern and commitment cannot be terminated by some change in or revelation about the object of that concern or commitment. We are inclined to accept 'I felt affection for her so long as I thought she was pure and innocent', but not 'I was really concerned for her welfare as long as I thought she was pure and innocent'. Being genuinely concerned or committed seems to involve a willingness on my part to extend that concern or commitment even if I have been mistaken about the person with regard to some feature of her that led to the concern, and even if that person

ceases to have those features which led me to be concerned or committed in the first place.[12]

This, though plausible, cannot be quite right, for on Newton-Smith's analysis it is difficult to see how I could ever give up a commitment without it being the case that I never was committed in the first place. But we can and do distinguish between those who had a commitment and have now given it up and those who never had a commitment at all. We need not, I think, go so far as to say that 'love is not love which alters when it alteration finds', but only that love is not love which allows in advance that it will so alter. The love which shows that it will alter when it alteration finds is at best sentimentality, at worst opportunistic. (Of course, the reasons which one cites for giving up a commitment will cast light on whether one was committed at all. Thus 'I was committed to her as long as I thought she was an heiress' is highly dubious. 'I was committed to her as long as I thought she was pure and innocent' is, I think, not so dubious.) What is at least necessary is that one should not be prepared to say *now* 'I will love her as long as she is pure and innocent, but no longer'.

I turn now to a somewhat bizarre element in Parfit's talk of ideals. Parfit portrays the Russian nobleman as one who 'finds' that his ideals have faded, as one who 'loses' his ideals when circumstances and fortune change. What is bizarre in this talk is emphasised by the following extract from Alison Lurie's novel *Love and Friendship*:

> 'But, Will, promise me something.'
> 'Sure.'
> 'Promise me you'll never be unfaithful to me.'
> Silence.
> Emily raised her head, 'You won't promise?' she said incredulously.
> 'I can't, Emily. How can I promise how I'll feel for the next ten years? You want me to lie to you? You could change. I could meet somebody.'
> Emily pulled away. 'Don't you have any principles?' she asked.[13]

The trouble with the inappropriately named Will and the Russian nobleman in Parfit's example is that it is doubtful whether either man has any genuine principles at all. Each is portrayed as almost infinitely malleable, as one whose principles will alter in accordance with changing circumstances. The point about a moral principle, however, is that it must serve in some sense to rule out certain options at all. In his article 'Actions and Consequences', John Casey refers us to the example of Addison's Cato who, when offered life, liberty and the friendship of Caesar if he will surrender and is asked to name his terms, replies:

> Bid him disband his legions,
> Restore the Commonwealth to liberty
> Submit his actions to the public censure
> And stand the judgement of a Roman Senate.
> Bid him do this and Cato is his friend.[14]

The genuine principles which Cato has determine that certain options will not ultimately be options at all for him. To say this, of course, is not to deny that life and liberty are attractive and desirable to him. Obviously he is, in large part, admirable precisely because they are attractive to him and yet he manages to resist their allure. The point is rather that not *any* sort of life is desirable. The sort of life he would, of necessity, lead after surrender – a life without honour – is not ultimately attractive to him, and that it is not attractive is something which springs from his having the principles he does have. What Cato values above all else is honour and his refusal to surrender to Caesar is a refusal to lead a life without honour.

By contrast, when the Russian nobleman draws up a legal document giving away his inheritance, we may suspect that he is concerned not with an honourable life or with a life which he now conceives of as honourable, but rather with his present principle. Where Cato values a certain sort of life, the Russian nobleman values a certain principle. It is this which is problematic and which generates, I believe, the bizarre talk of ideals fading. For Cato's adherence to his principles is strengthened, if not guaranteed, by the fact that he treats a certain sort of life as an end in itself and adopts the principles he does adopt because they lead to the end. The Russian nobleman, however, is portrayed more as a man who finds the principle important than as a man who finds the life to which the principle leads important. Obviously, in either case there may be temptation and inner struggle, but the temptation is less likely to be resisted by the Russian nobleman than by Cato, for the nobleman will find his principle undermined and threatened by the prospect of affluence, which is attractive to him. His ideals will fade. For Cato, on the other hand, things are not so simple. He is not faced with a choice between two things, each of which he finds attractive. The fact that he treats a life of honour as an end in itself precludes his finding life attractive under *any* circumstances. For him, life will ultimately be attractive and desirable only where it can be conducted honourably. Nevertheless, he finds life attractive and desirable, but this means only that if he surrenders he will have *sacrificed* his ideals, not that his ideals will have faded. Thus, the nobleman is a victim, waiting for and guarding against attack upon his principles; Cato is an agent who may sacrifice his principles after a struggle, but he is not someone who would find that they had altered.

In conclusion, then, the claim that the marriage vow is either impossible or improper is false. It is possible to commit oneself unconditionally because commitment is analogous to a statement of intention, not to a prediction or a piece of clairvoyance. It is proper, since if we refuse to allow such unconditional commitment, we run the risk of failing to distinguish between, on the one hand, sentimentality and commitment, and admiration and commitment on the other. Further, it is simply not true that I am helpless in circumstances in which I find my commitment wavering. This is because my principles will initially serve to modify my view of the opportunities which present themselves, and I simply will not see certain things as constituting success because my principles are such as to preclude their being consititutive of success. In this way, my principles determine what is to count as a benefit and what is to count as an opportunity. As Shakespeare has it:

> Some glory in their birth, some in their skill,
> Some in their wealth, some in their body's force,
> Some in their garments though new fangled ill:
> Some in their hawks and hounds, some in their horse.
> And every humour has his adjunct pleasure,
> Wherein it finds a joy above the rest,
> But these particulars are not my measure,
> All these I better in one general best.

Thy love is better than high birth to me,
Richer than wealth, prouder than garments cost,
Of more delight than hawks and horses be:
And having these of all men's pride I boast.
Wretched in this alone, that thou may'st take
All this away, and me most wretched make.[15,16]

Part II
The Politics of Love

6
To Have and to Hold: Liberalism and the Marriage Contract

The starting point of this chapter is a question about the nature and extent of modern liberalism. Specifically, it addresses the question; 'How comprehensive can liberalism be, and how much of social and moral life can it aspire to explain?' The question is prompted by a (somewhat crude) distinction between historical and modern liberalism. Historically, liberals have usually set themselves rather modest aims and have distinguished between the scope of political philosophy and the scope of moral philosophy. Both Locke and Hume differentiate between the requirements of political justice and the prior, and independent, dictates of morality. They construe politics as being necessitated by our imperfect moral nature. As Sandel points out:

> For Hume, justice cannot be the first virtue of social institutions, and in some cases it is doubtfully a virtue at all . . . Insofar as mutual benevolence and enlarged affections could be cultivated more widely, the need for 'the cautious, jealous virtue of justice' would diminish in proportion, and mankind would be the better for it.[1]

More recently, however, political liberalism has expanded into a theory which includes both moral and political concerns. Thus Rawls's early liberalism aspires to provide an account of moral and political life, in which all institutions are subject to the same conditions of justification, and all are called to the tribunal of justice. Where Hume's political philosophy forms a subdivision of his moral philosophy, Rawls's political philosophy embraces and explains moral philosophy. Thus, *A Theory of Justice* is not simply an account of justice in social institutions, but a general account of the primacy of justice in all relationships. As one writer has put it: '*A Theory of Justice* opens with the electric declaration that "justice is the first virtue of social institutions". By the time the next 600 pages have been traversed a reader must be forgiven for thinking that justice is the only virtue of social institutions *and of the individuals who compose them*'[2] (my emphasis). This distinction between broad and narrow interpretations of liberalism generates questions about how successful liberalism can be in explaining personal relationships such as relationships of love and, particularly, of marriage. Marriage is an interesting case because it straddles the moral and political realms, being both a private (perhaps the most private) relationship and a political institution which is legally endorsed.

One of the aims of this chapter is to examine the morality of marriage, but also, and more generally, to assess its place in the liberal tradition. I shall use the example of marriage to display what seem to me to be profound difficulties for a more extensive liberal theory, but at the same time I shall suggest that (at least some) feminist responses to these difficulties have been misguided. The structure of the chapter is as follows: ignoring controversies about the correct definition of liberalism (first catch your hare), I shall pick out two of its central features – *contract* and the *public/private distinction*. These features are not only crucial to liberalism, but also (and most importantly for my purposes) they are the ones which, jointly, have been thought to pose problems for liberal conceptions of marriage. I shall discuss the nature of these problems and suggest some ways in which feminism has misunderstood them. In particular, I shall argue that at least some feminist suspicion of marriage is unwarranted and should be replaced by feminist suspicion of liberalism. Finally, I shall propose an alternative understanding of marriage – one which may not immediately commend itself to feminists, but which may provide a better understanding of marriage as a moral ideal, and a warning against the more extensive forms of liberalism favoured by modern philosophers such as Rawls.

Contract

The idea of contract has been closely associated with liberalism from earliest to latest days. From John Locke to John Rawls the importance of contract has never been far from the liberal mind, and despite grave difficulties surrounding the status of the contract (as hypothetical or actual, tacit or explicit), the idea retains its appeal. In a seminal article on the subject, Jeremy Waldron has identified contract as *the* theoretical foundation of liberal thought. Not, of course, in the sense that all liberals subscribe to it but, and as he says, 'because it expresses in a clear and provocative form a view most liberals do share: that the social order must be one that can be justified to the people who have to live under it'.[3] The guiding thought here is that the social order must be intelligible and justifiable to each and every person in the society. In this respect, liberals show their credentials as descendants of enlightenment thinkers. They share with the latter a desire for intelligibility and order. They require that the world (the natural world, the political world and the social world) should be made intelligible or *transparent*. It should not be shrouded in mystery, nor should it, in the political case, depend upon mythology, mystification or the Platonic 'noble lie'. 'Liberals demand that the social order should be capable of explaining itself at the tribunal of each person's understanding.'

Against this background, liberal commitment to contract is unsurprising: it is an obvious answer to the demand for legitimacy, intelligibility or transparency in at least two senses: first, the fact that an individual has entered into a contract (or would enter into a contract) tends to imply that the arrangement is legitimate. Second, and conversely, the fact that an arrangement is one to which no one would, or even could, consent suggests that it is illegitimate. The contractual account of social institutions serves to legitimize those institutions. Thus, in the case of marriage, a contractual account legitimizes in a way in which a non-contractual account would not. Waldron's argument explains both the general appeal of contract in the liberal tradition and, by extension, the specific appeal of a contractarian analysis of marriage. By speaking of marriage in a contractual manner, the liberal is bringing it to the tribunal of public scrutiny.

Public and private

All this would be comparatively unproblematic (though not uncontroversial) were it not for the fact that liberalism is also committed to a public/private distinction. 'Privacy constitutes what is perhaps the central idea of liberalism,'[4] says Steven Lukes, and the implication of this is clear. Although everything public must be rendered transparent, not everything is public, and those things which are not public need not explain themselves at the tribunal of public scrutiny. There is, it seems, still room for mythology, mystification and 'the noble lie', but that room is a private room. Most worryingly, it is the marriage bedroom, for when liberals speak of privacy they tend not to mean the privacy of solitude, but the privacy of domestic life, where marriage and the family constitute the paradigm examples of private life. Both historically and in modern liberalism, 'the writ of the state runs out at the gate of the family home'.

The upshot of this is that liberalism, in its attitude to marriage, seems to be somewhat Janus-faced. Liberal attempts to analyse marriage on the contractual model are not simply denied but refuted by liberal insistence on construing marriage and the family as paradigmatic examples of the private. Moreover, there is no easy way out of the difficulty, for both contract and the public/private distinction are central to liberal thinking. They are not optional extras which can be dispensed with when the going gets tough. To deny that marriage is private implies the panopticism of a Bentham:

> The whole kingdom, the whole globe itself, will become a gymnasium, in which every man exercises himself before the eyes of every other man. Every gesture, every turn of limb or feature, in those whose motions have a visible impact on the general happiness, will be noticed and marked down.[5]

On the other hand, to insist that marriage is private implies that it is not, after all, an area in which questions of power and legitimacy arise or, at the very least, it implies that when they do arise, they are not important. Genuine power struggles, it seems, are to be distinguished from mere domestic squabbles and, as Waldron points out 'to the extent that this line of thought is taken seriously, liberals leave themselves open to the charge of being less than wholehearted about the legitimation of *all* structures of power in modern society'.[6]

And so they do, for it is at this point that liberalism has traditionally encountered its most vociferous feminist critics. The distinction between public and private answers to the reality of many women's lives (they know there to be such a distinction, and they know that they are on the private side of it), but it answers in a way which confirms their worst fears about the patriarchal structure of liberal societies. Liberal insistence on the distinction between the personal and the political masks the fact that 'personal' or 'private' problems often stand in need of political solutions. Indeed, one feminist writer goes further, suggesting that 'the dichotomy between the private and the public is central to almost two centuries of feminist writing and political struggle; it is, ultimately, what the feminist movement is about'.[7]

My scope here is (mercifully) more limited than the *raison d'être* of the entire feminist movement. What I want to suggest, however, is that in the particular case of the liberal conception of marriage, the problem is less to do with the public/private distinction than it is to do with the idea of contract and the associated requirement of transparency. Feminists have often been critical of liberalism's alleged refusal to bring marriage into the public sphere. I shall suggest, however, that they ought to be less concerned about this and more concerned about the requirement of transparency, which is built into liberalism's commitment to contract.

Liberalism and the marriage contract

If we accept Waldron's claim that the idea of contract is the theoretical foundation of liberalism, then the charge against liberals is that they are unable or unwilling to extend that idea into the domestic realm. If liberals are interested in legitimizing power structures, and if marriages are power structures, and if power structures can best be legitimized via the notion of contract, then marriages ought to be construed on the contractual model. And so they have been. Far from refusing to understand marriage as a contract, liberals have been largely incapable of understanding it in any other way. The reasons for this are two-fold: first, there is the consideration of transparency appealed to by Waldron; second, there is the relationship which liberals believe to hold between persons and their bodies. These two reasons answer (roughly) to modern and historical liberalism respectively. In the history of political theory, the contractual account has been closely associated with the belief that persons own a property in their own bodies, whereas in modern accounts the contract model is generated by the requirement of transparency. Carole Pateman describes the case as follows:

> The conception of marriage as essentially contractual is part of the theoretical stock of liberalism . . . the keystone of the contractarian view of marriage is the doctrine that individuals have a right in one another's bodies. The right follows from a conception of individuals as owning the property they possess in their persons and bodies; one individual can thus have rightful access to, or sexual use of, the body of another only with the consent or agreement of, or through a contract with the property owner. The marriage contract establishes legitimate access to the body of a spouse.[8]

The belief that persons have a property in their bodies has its genesis in John Locke, whose *Second Treatise* tells us that 'Though the Earth, and all inferior Creatures be common to all Men, yet every Man has a Property in his own Person'. Marriage, moreover, is to be understood as 'a Voluntary compact between Man and Woman', which consists chiefly in 'such a Communion and Right in One another's Bodies, as is necessary to its chief End, Procreation'.[9] Moreover, this contractual analysis is reiterated and extended by Kant, who construes all sexual relations as fundamentally exploitative – as instances of treating another person as the means to one's own end. 'Matrimony,' he tells us, 'is an agreement between two persons by which they grant each other equal reciprocal rights, each of them undertaking to surrender the whole of their person to the other with a complete right of disposal over it.'[10] Thus the contractual understanding of marriage springs both from the requirement of transparency referred to by Waldron, and from the conception of persons as having a property in their own bodies.

These two distinct foundations of the contractual analysis generate distinct moral justifications: where considerations of transparency are appealed to, they reflect our belief that contracts are fair to the extent that they have been freely chosen. On the other hand, where the appeal is to persons as property owners, this reflects our feeling that contracts are fair to the extent that the benefits accruing from them are mutual and equal. In other words, we may ask two questions about the fairness of a contract: 'Was it voluntarily entered into?' and 'Are its terms fair?' To see that these are distinct, we need only remind ourselves that even under conditions of fairness, individuals may agree to terms which are less than fair, and conversely that conditions of unfairness may deliver fair terms. Thus:

> we may think of the morality of contracts as consisting of two related yet distinguishable ideals. One is the ideal of autonomy, which sees a contract as an act of will, whose morality consists in the voluntary character of the transaction. The other is the ideal of reciprocity, which sees a contract as an instrument of mutual benefit, whose morality depends on the underlying fairness of the exchange.[11]

In the first case, it is the mere fact that the agreement was freely entered into which generates its moral justification, whereas in the second case some independent criterion of fairness in exchange operates to determine the morality of the contract.

The marriage contract has been attacked as offending against both ideals; in his 1825 *Appeal* William Thompson makes much of the fact that, from the woman's point of view, the contract is not freely entered into. Social and legal constraints in nineteenth-century Britain served to make marriage an inescapable necessity for women: 'Each man yokes a woman to his establishment and calls it a contract. Audacious falsehood! . . . A contract implies the *voluntary assent* of both the contracting parties.'[12] On the other hand, John Stuart Mill's *Subjection of Women* concentrates on the unfairness in the *terms* of the contract:

> Casuists may say that the obligation of obedience stops short of participation in crime, but it certainly extends to everything else. She [the wife] can do no act whatever but by his [the husband's] permission, at least tacit. She can acquire no property but for him; the instant it becomes hers, it becomes *ipso facto* his. In this respect the wife's position under the common law of England is worse than that of slaves in the laws of many countries.[13]

It is important to remember, however, that these different criticisms answer to different moral justifications of contract generally and of the marriage contract in particular. The former refers to the ideal of autonomy; the latter to the ideal of reciprocity. In the next two sections I shall discuss each in turn and try to draw some conclusions about liberal commitment to the idea of contract and about the appropriate feminist response to it.

Contract and autonomy

When contract answers to the ideal of autonomy its moral justification lies in the fact that it is a voluntary transaction. That an individual freely and voluntarily agreed, serves to justify the contractual arrangement entered into and, conversely, where a contract was not freely entered into, that, as Thompson points out, serves to unjustify. And Thompson's criticism of nineteenth-century marriage implies that all would be well if only women were free. To the extent that this is so, he subscribes to the contractual account based on the ideal of autonomy: he sees the institution of marriage as legitimized by its contractual status. Two questions therefore arise: 'Does marriage have the status of a contract even when women are free?' and 'Are contracts legitimized by the fact of being freely entered into?' In each case, the answer given will have consequences for liberalism generally and not merely for liberalism's conception of marriage.

On the first question I shall be brief, since this topic is thoroughly discussed elsewhere.[14] The crucial point, however, is this: political theory, particularly modern political theory, regularly blurs the distinction between contract and consent, implying that all consent is consent to a contractual arrangement. This, however, is misleading: consent may be consent to an externally defined status, as it is in the case of marriage, even where marriage is freely entered into. Pateman writes: 'The conclusion to be drawn from the feminist critique of the marriage contract is precisely that it is a fiction. It is called a contract between a man and a woman; the reality is that they consent to the patriarchally ascribed status of superior husband and subordinate wife.'[15] Unlike genuine contracts, the marriage contract contains terms which are unalterable and which vest in the parties a hierarchical and externally determined status. (Thus, for example, Mill found to his cost that he could not dictate the terms of the contract into which he entered on marrying Harriet Taylor. Nothing *he* did could alter the fact of his status as superior husband and her status as subordinate wife.) I shall suggest later that this aspect of marriage has a positive as well as a negative side. For now, I simply note that, *pace* Thompson, we cannot secure the contractual status of marriage simply by removing social pressures.

Does voluntary agreement nevertheless legitimize? The idea of contract which answers to the ideal of autonomy suggests that it does.The simple fact that an individual freely agreed to an arrangement confers moral legitimacy on that arrangement. Indeed, this thought reflects some of our deepest intuitions about the importance of autonomy and of respect for persons. However harsh the terms of an agreement, however disadvantaged an individual may be as a result of them, they are at least partly justified by the thought that they are terms to which the agent freely and voluntarily agreed. This thought, however, raises the question: 'What constitutes a voluntary agreement?' As Thompson implies, not any utterance of the words 'I consent' is sufficient to guarantee voluntariness. Such words may be uttered at gun point, or (more usually) under severe social pressure, but even where neither of these constraints operates, it is doubtful whether legitimacy is guaranteed in quite the way required. This is partly because questions of legitimacy arise about the terms of the contract, as well as about the conditions under which it is made. However, it is also partly because the ideal of autonomy which is being appealed to here is a wholly unrealistic one. 'However strictly one defines the requirements of a voluntary agreement, the fact that different persons are situated differently will ensure that some differences of power and knowledge persist, allowing even voluntary agreements to be influenced by factors arbitrary from a moral point of view.'[16] In entering into agreements people may be misinformed or misled. They may be bad judges of their own needs, bad judges of risk, or simply ignorant of the value of the goods being exchanged. To say this is not to deny that there is any such thing as a voluntary agreement, it is rather to insist that voluntary agreements are not legitimized by the mere fact of their voluntariness. Moreover, and most importantly for my purposes, it drives a wedge between agreements which are not freely entered into and agreements which are not legitimized even though they are freely entered into. In the case of marriage, much emphasis has been placed on the former – on the fact that women are not (or at least were not) free to decline marriage, but considerations of unequal knowledge and power suggest that even if they were free, it would not follow that the agreement would be morally justified.

This thought has wide-ranging consequences for liberalism generally. The original thesis – that contract provides the theoretical foundation of liberal political philosophy – depends ultimately on appeal to the concept of autonomy. At root, the claim is that contracts are justified by *fully autonomous* utterances of the words 'I consent', but full autonomy is vitiated by the contingencies of real life – by inequalities of knowledge, or of power, by social setting and psychological characteristics. In brief, full autonomy is a chimera, not something which operates in the world.[17] However, if the agreement itself can justify only on the assumption that it is fully autonomous, and if full autonomy is not possible, then attention must turn away from the *fact* of the agreement and towards the *terms* of the agreement. In other words, we must examine the morality of contracts by reference to the ideal of reciprocity.

Contract and reciprocity

As has already been noted, liberals are no strangers to the ideal of reciprocity as regards marriage: 'the keystone of the contractarian view of marriage is the doctrine that individuals have a right in one another's bodies . . . the marriage contract establishes legitimate access to the body of a spouse.' Indeed, in the Kantian scheme of things, at least one feminist objection to marriage is turned on its head, for:

> the feminist complains that the man treats the woman as a sexual object. Kant suggests that the complaint is more deep lying than this. According to him, both the man and the woman treat each other as things. This suggests that the feminist argument that sex takes on an exploitative form in modern society might best be reformulated not as an instance of the inhumanity of man towards woman, but as an instance of the general inhumanity of man (i.e. human beings in general) towards man.[18]

Again, the point can be generalized: liberal belief that persons have a property in their own bodies generates a conception of sexual relations as the reciprocal lease of the sexual organs, and this in turn encourages a view of the marriage relationship as contractual and to be justified by appeal to the ideal of reciprocity. Put bluntly, liberals are committed to construing marriage as a bargain, a kind of business relationship. Given the fact that voluntariness cannot, on its own, legitimize the bargain (given that the ideal of autonomy will not do all the moral work), the most plausible liberal strategy is to ensure that the terms of the bargain are fair. Marriage will thus be justified by appeal to the ideal of reciprocity, if not by appeal to the ideal of autonomy. This, I take it, is Mill's strategy in *The Subjection of Women*. Whilst recognizing that the circumstances under which women enter into marriage are not circumstances of fairness, Mill takes as his primary focus the unfairness in the terms of the Victorian marriage contract. He urges legal equality and changes to suffrage and property legislation which will serve to make a woman more than the mere 'bond servant' of her husband.

In criticizing this analysis, I certainly do not wish to undermine the importance of Mill's strategy, much less to suggest that he was wrong to seek legal equality for married women. What I would point out, however, is that this is not merely a *strategy* for liberals if liberalism is indeed committed to contract as its theoretical foundation. The requirement of reciprocity occurs not only in Mill's attack on legal institutions, but also in his statement of the *moral* ideal of marriage. He is committed not only to fair transfer and bargain in the legal area, but also to fair transfer and bargain as a statement of what marriage ideally should be.[19] His discussion of the moral ideal of marriage concentrates on notions of reciprocity, equality of powers and justice, just as much as does his attack on Victorian legislation governing marriage. In this respect, far from being guilty of consigning marriage to the private side of the public/private distinction, Mill is more properly charged with dragging it wholesale into the public arena.

I began this chapter by pointing to a dilemma which appears to cause trouble for liberal understandings of marriage. The dilemma is that liberals purport to require the legitimation of all sources of power, and all social institutions. However, by their insistence on adopting an untenable public/private distinction, they deny that marriages are the scenes of important power struggles and legitimation crises. They thus 'leave themselves open to the charge of being less than wholehearted about the legitimation of all structures of power in modern society'. But the real problem, I suggest, is somewhat different. Far from being loath to make marriage a publicly justifiable institution, modern liberals, from Mill onwards, see it as exhaustively explicable in these terms, whether it is considered as a legal arrangement or as a moral one.

Some, of course, will not object to this conclusion. In her book *Parallel Lives*, Phyllis Rose remarks:

> Like Mill, I believe marriage to be the primary political experience in which most of us engage as adults, and so I am interested in the management of power between men and women in that microcosmic relationship . . . People who find this a chilling way to talk about one of our most treasured human bonds will object that 'power struggle' is a flawed circumstance into which relationships fall when love fails. I would counter by pointing out the human tendency to invoke love at moments when we want to disguise transactions involving power. Like the aged Lear handing over his kingdom to his daughters, when we resign power, or assume new power, we insist it is not happening and demand to be talked to about love.[20]

As a statement of psychological fact, this may often be true. Moreover, since Mary Wollstonecraft, it has been a thought which has informed much feminist suspicion of the analysis of marriage in terms of love, for love is often the consolatory bone thrown to women to disguise the fact of their powerlessness. What is worrying, however, is the suggestion that marriage is by its very nature a power struggle, or that this bargaining model is a statement of what marriage (as a moral ideal) essentially is. Rushing in where angels fear to tread, I would suggest that it is the bargaining model and the concomitant insistence on transparency which forces the tragedy of Lear. The tragic flaw in Lear is not his failure to recognize that he is engaged in a transfer of power. His fault, rather, lies in his insistence on construing love on the bargaining model – on perceiving love as something to be offered in exchange for power:

> Which of you shall we say doth love us most?
> That we our largest bounty may extend
> Where nature doth with merit challenge?

Thus prompting Cordelia's response: 'What shall Cordelia do? Love and be silent.' When Cordelia refuses to play the bargaining game, when she insists that her love is not to be measured, bought or sold, the tragic implications of the bargaining model become clear. But the bargaining model is precisely the one which informs liberalism's attitude to marriage and to human relationships generally. Why is this unsatisfactory?

Earlier in the chapter I made reference to the criticism that marriage is not a contract at all, but an example of consent to hierarchical and unalterable status, and I suggested that this consideration might turn out to have a positive as well as a negative side. It seems to me that what is characteristic of the marriage relationship is precisely that it is a commitment to unalterable status and not a bargain. Within the liberal tradition, this status is construed as either superior or inferior, but there is no reason in general why this should be so. Familial relationships are also relationships of status, but they are not thereby hierarchical. They are merely unalterable. My sister is always and unalterably my sister, but she is not thereby superior or subordinate. I owe to her more than justice requires (more than the terms of a fair bargain would dictate), but I owe it not on account of any agreement I have made, nor on account of any contract I have entered into. I owe it simply because she is my sister. As an ideal, the marriage relationship approximates to this model: it attempts, by voluntary agreement, to confer unalterable status. Most importantly, it is an attempt, through voluntary agreement, to reject the bargaining model. Victorian feminists objected that the bargain of marriage was not voluntary, or that, if voluntary, it was not fair. But the real point is that it is not a bargain at all. It is a commitment to giving up the language of bargains. Of course, commitments may fade, but the fact that we do not always honour our commitments does not, in itself, translate commitment into contract.[21] This raises a further point about the status of modern liberalism and its requirement of transparency.

In this chapter it has been suggested that liberalism is at fault in construing marriage as a contract, and that the contractual model may be generated either by appeal to transparency or by the belief that persons own their bodies. Liberals, however, place great emphasis on the need for transparency, and in so far as the contract model was designed to render institutions transparent, liberals are therefore committed to providing a public explanation of the nature of marriage. In doing this they respond in part to some major feminist concerns about marriage. Feminists who claim that marriages are the scenes of important power struggles cannot properly complain when requirements of transparency are made to apply to marriage (as they often are in modern liberalism). Yet there is a danger in complying with this strategy. In *Ethics and the Limits of Philosophy* Bernard Williams remarks:

> It is one aspiration, that social and ethical relations should not essentially rest on ignorance and misunderstanding of what they are, and quite another that all the beliefs and principles involved in them should be explicitly stated. That these are two different things is obvious with personal relations, where to hope that they do not rest on deceit and error is merely decent, but to think that their basis can be made totally explicit is idiocy.[22]

To construe marriage on a contractual model is to imply that all the beliefs and principles which inform it can be so explained. Whether the contractual model takes its force from a requirement of transparency or from a view of persons as owners of their bodies, the result is the same: marriages must be totally explicable.

My conclusion, then, is this: feminists have often urged that marriage should be construed as a public relationship. They rightly claim that marriages are the scenes of important power struggles and insist that this be recognized in liberalism's treatment of marriage. In some respects, however, liberals have shown too much rather than too little enthusiasm in responding to that request. They have presented feminists with a dilemma: incorporate marriage into the liberal scheme of things by rendering it totally explicable, or stop complaining. But when offered a dilemma, we do not have to impale ourselves on one or other horn. We can reject the dilemma entirely. We can admit that marriages are the scenes of important power struggles without supposing that they are to be analysed in exclusively contractual terms. In doing this, we remind ourselves of the limits of liberalism. We remind ourselves of Hume's claim that the principles of political philosophy are necessary because human beings are frail and imperfect. Where marriages go well they are informed by principles which are not totally explicable and are not, at root, the principles of justice. Justice and the requirements of transparency are needed because things are likely to go wrong. They are not the principles which give an exhaustive account of what happens when things go right. They are, in brief, political principles, not moral ideals.[23]

7
Different Voices, Still Lives: Problems in the Ethics of Care

> The moral imperative ... [for] women is an injunction to care, a responsibility to discern and alleviate the 'real and recognizable trouble' of this world. For men, the moral imperative appears rather as an injunction to respect the rights of others and thus to protect from interference the rights to life and self-fulfilment ... The standard of moral judgement that informs [women's] assessment of the self is a standard of relationship, an ethic of nurturance, responsibility, and care.[1]

Since the publication of Carol Gilligan's *In A Different Voice* feminist theorists have embraced a distinction between an ethic of justice and an ethic of care. Moral theories couched in terms of rights, justice and abstract rationality have given way to moral theories which emphasize care, compassion and contextualization, and it is widely argued that these latter values reflect women's lives and women's concerns far more accurately than do the abstract and atomistic values inherent in, for example, John Rawls's theory of justice, or Kantian conceptions of morality generally. As the quotation demonstrates, Gilligan's account, which is based on the findings of empirical psychological research, asserts that the justice perspective is predominantly male, the care perspective predominantly female, but moral and political philosophy have ignored the findings of psychology and in consequence have emphasized the (male) perspective of justice to the near exclusion of (female) conceptions of care. In this respect they have shown a distinct gender bias, and feminists now urge the need for rectification and an acknowledgement of the moral (as well as the psychological) importance of the language of care.

However, in urging a move from abstraction to contextualization, and from considerations of justice to considerations of care, feminist theorists tread on dangerous ground. From Aristotle to Hegel, woman's 'special' nature or 'different' voice has been used as the primary justification for her confinement to the domestic realm and her exclusion from political life. Thus, notoriously, Hegel tells us that 'When women hold the helm of government, the state is at once in jeopardy, because women regulate their actions not by the demands of universality but by arbitrary inclinations and opinions'.[2] Similarly, Rousseau declared that 'a perfect man and a perfect woman should no more be alike in mind than in face',[3] and western political philosophy is replete with similar examples of arguments which move from the assertion of woman's different, caring nature to the conclusion that she is unfitted for public life. Against this background, the aspiration to deploy an ethic of care in pursuit of feminist ends must be treated with considerable caution.

The converse also applies: difference theorists not only appear to ally themselves with arguments which have been used to women's disadvantage, they also, and at the same time, distance themselves from a long tradition of feminist theory and practice – a tradition which has embraced abstract rights as the most important single means of escaping from oppression. As Anne Phillips puts it:

> The liberal language of individual rights and freedoms has a tremendous resonance for women . . . much of the personal impetus towards a feminist politics is to do with claiming the space to choose who and what you are – not to be defined, contained and dictated by notions of 'woman'.[4]

Thus, difference theory in general, and the ethics of care in particular, raise serious problems for feminists. My aim in this chapter is to draw attention to those problems and to suggest ways in which they might be avoided or overcome. Specifically, I shall argue that on the individual level the ethics of care runs the risk of adopting too unitary and static a conception of woman's identity, and of ignoring the conflicts inherent in women's lives. Connectedly, I shall suggest that on the political level the concept of care is too narrow to do the work required of it: considerations of care are largely limited to those whom we know, and are problematic if extended to the wider world of unknown others which is the central sphere of politics. Finally, however, I shall suggest that the ethics of care does identify important defects in justice theory. If interpreted not as a theory about the activity of caring, but as a theory of the passivity of life, the ethics of care may provide the foundations for a political philosophy which recognizes our need for just treatment in virtue of our inherent vulnerability. This conclusion serves, moreover, to suggest that we should not interpret 'the ethics of justice' and 'the ethics of care' as distinct and alternative ethical systems, but rather as complementary facets of any realistic account of morality.

Care, difference and politics

There are two features of an ethic of care to which I wish to draw attention. The first is its emphasis on the differences which divide people rather than the similarities which unite; the second is the centrality it accords to small-scale, face-to-face relationships. Each of these features promises to mitigate the impersonality associated with an ethic of justice but, I shall argue, the price is high. As we have seen, emphasis on difference threatens political exclusion. It has uncomfortable associations with the arguments of the great dead philosophers, who claimed that woman's different nature justified her confinement to a separate domestic sphere, distinct from the sphere of politics. Moreover, emphasis on small, face-to-face relationships compounds the difficulty when once we recognize that political problems are characteristically large-scale. Typically, they do not arise at the level of individual relationships, and therefore an ethic which concentrates on the small scale may have little to contribute to their solution. At the very least, argument will be needed to show whether and how the features characteristic of small-scale relationships may be extended in such a way as to inform political practice. First, then, an ethic of care is an ethic which emphasizes difference rather than similarity. References to this feature can be found throughout feminist philosophy, and I shall mention just two places where the argument is prominent.

In her article 'Liberty and Equality from a Feminist Perspective',

Virginia Held asserts: 'We give birth, and you do not. This is a radical difference, and the fact that you lack this capacity may distort your whole view of the social realm.'⁵ And similarly Cheshire Calhoun argues that:

> Too much talk about our similarities as moral selves, and too little talk about our differences has its moral dangers . . . Unless moral theory shifts its priority to knowledgeable discussion of human differences – particularly differences tied to gender, race, class and power – lists and rank orderings of basic human interests and rights as well as the political deployment of those lists are likely to be sexist, racist and classist.⁶

An ethic of care, then, unlike an ethic of justice, takes the differences between people as central and as the appropriate starting point for both moral and political philosophy.

Secondly, and connectedly, an ethic of care concentrates on the particularities of actual relationships rather than the dictates of universal reason. Kittay and Meyers draw the contrast as follows:

> A morality of rights and abstract reason begins with a moral agent who is separate from others, and who independently elects moral principles to obey. In contrast, a morality of responsibility and care begins with a self who is enmeshed in a network of relations to others, and whose moral deliberation aims to maintain these relations.⁷

Unlike an ethic of justice, an ethic of care emphasizes the extent to which people are at least partly constituted by their relationships with those around them. It is these relationships which define their moral responsibilities and which should therefore inform our discussions of moral and political life. Emphasis on the differences which divide people (particularly the differences which divide men and women), and on the importance of actual relationships as constitutive of individual identity and moral responsibility, are therefore central to the distinction between an ethic of justice and an ethic of care. There are, however, two ways in which these features are problematic. On the individual level, they imply a conception of female identity which is altogether too simplistic and unitary; and on a political level, they assume a kind of society wholly different from that which exists in the post-industrial world of the late twentieth century.

Insistence on female difference, specifically on the 'radical' differences which divide men and women, is often ambivalent between an assertion of biological difference, rooted in women's status as child-*bearers*, and an assertion of social difference, rooted in women's traditional role as child-*carers*. Proponents of the ethic of care tend to vacillate uneasily between the claim that women's biological nature as child-bearers renders them especially sensitive to considerations of care and compassion, and the claim that women's status as child-carers makes them more conscious of those considerations, but either way feminist politics is jeopardized, for the former account renders women prisoners of their own biology, and the latter advocates for all women a single, defining role which in fact only some women occupy.

Of course, in so far as an ethic of care points to the importance of virtues other than the virtue of justice, it is powerful and important. Held is surely right to note that equality and justice are only two virtues amongst many and that, in ordinary life, the claims of care and compassion may be more central and more compelling. But she and others go further, implying a deep and defining connection between an ethic of care and women's identity. For her, the specification of women's identity contains essential reference to birth, care and the raising of children. The same is not true of men, and this difference, it is claimed, generates a dramatically different perspective on moral problems and moral responsibilities. Thus Held concludes:

> When we dare to give voice to how we think the world ought to be, we can imagine that whether one adopts the point of view of those who give birth or whether one does not may radically change one's perspective on most of what is most important.[8]

Well, we can imagine that, but it is a risky activity and not, on the whole, one which has delivered much by way of improvement in women's political condition. On the contrary, it is emphasis on common humanity *despite* difference which has served women far better, since it has provided standards of impartiality which are necessary in the pursuit of equality.[9]

There is, however, a further implication of the ethic of care which I wish to note here. This is that, in addition to emphasizing differences *between* the moral perspectives of men and women, it also threatens to ignore the acute conflicts of identity which occur *within* the lives of many women. Thus, while Held correctly notes the extent to which considerations of care inform women's moral judgements, she is silent on the extent to which care, compassion and the raising of children also generate conflicts within women's lives as they strive, for example, to combine domestic duties with professional duties. In the modern world, being a mother is only one role which is occupied by many women, and this role must be reconciled with other, often incompatible, roles. Again, this is not to deny that, for example, considerations of compassion ought to enter into the workplace, or into wider society. It is simply to note that care is a problematic concept: at the individual level, it may become 'chronic self-denial', whilst at the political level it may serve as an inadequate (and financially expedient) substitute for justice. Put bluntly, the identification of women with care has nostalgic overtones and threatens to result in a dangerously romantic conception of domesticity. Romantic because it idealizes the maternal role, while remaining almost wholly silent as to its frustrations; dangerous because it implies a conceptual link between maternal virtues and political virtues. In fact, however, the disanalogies between the two are quite striking, and it is far from clear how maternal virtues are related to political ones. Specifically, mother–child relationships are characterized by an intimacy wholly lacking in relationships between citizens. As Mary Dietz has pointed out:

> the bond among citizens is not like the love between a mother and child, for citizens are not intimately, but politically involved with each other . . . citizens do not, because they cannot, relate to one another as brother does to brother, or mother does to child. We look in the wrong place for a model of democratic citizenship if we look to the family (even when we have carefully defined the family.[10]

Moreover, the relationship between mother and child, unlike the relationship between citizens, is not one of equality, but one of hierarchy, and in this respect too the mother–child relationship is not straightforwardly analogous to the relationship between citizens. Maternal virtues are therefore different from citizen virtues both in respect of intimacy and in respect of hierarchy. Feminist emphasis on care and compassion thus generates three distinct but related worries: the first is that its emphasis on difference implies a view of women which, historically, has been associated with policies of political exclusion. The second is that it implies an over-simple, and static, view of female identity, which misdescribes women's role in modern life, and the third is that it appeals to an inappropriate analogy between familial and political relationships.

However, Dietz's contention that there is a difference of kind between familial and political relationships ignores the persuasive power of the analogy both for feminists and for communitarians, for feminists are not alone in urging that politics should be informed by the actual relationships which invest individuals' lives with meaning and significance, and it is here that the nostalgic nature of both feminism and (some forms of) communitarianism becomes most apparent. By urging the centrality of face-to-face relationships, proponents of the ethics of care hope to render political life an extension of family life. This may be an appropriate aim in societies which are small-scale, and where face-to-face relationships are the norm. But in large, anonymous, post-industrial societies the analogy becomes diminishingly useful or plausible. In brief, an ethic of care seems best suited to small-scale societies where face-to-face relationships are the norm, but these societies are not the ones which we now have. Modern society is large, sprawling and anonymous, and whilst we might wish that it were not so, the insistence on an ethic which emphasizes actual relationships may nevertheless appear nostalgic and untrue to the realities of modern life.

In this respect, the problems inherent in an ethic of care are akin to the problems encountered by those forms of socialism which emphasize the importance of small communities and the face-to-face relationships which they foster. Speaking about these forms of socialism David Miller notes:

> Socialism became a popular ideology precisely in response to the breakup of traditional communities under the impact of the industrial revolution. It became popular because it promised to restore the coherent moral life found in disappearing communities, whilst

at the same time providing all the material (and other) benefits of industrialization. But these two promises could never be fulfilled together. In industrial societies the appeal to community is always nostalgic and backward looking, whatever its proponents may think.[11]

And we may have a similar worry about the ethic of care, for in so far as this too promises to restore the coherence of moral life, it too is vulnerable to the charge of nostalgia and lack of realism about the facts of the modern world.

The theoretical worry which is generated by these thoughts is simply that, in the modern world, the concept of care is too weak to do the work required of it: unsupported by considerations of justice and equality, care may not extend reliably beyond the immediacy of one's own family, or group, or clan, to the wider world of unknown others. If identity and morality are constituted by actual relationships of care between particular people, they will not easily translate to the wider political problems of world hunger, poverty and war, which involve vast numbers of unknown people. Writing on this subject, Michael Ignatieff says:

> We recognize our humanity in our differences, in our individuality, our history, in the faithful discharge of our particular culture of obligations. There is no identity we can recognize in our universality. There is no such thing as love of the human race, only the love of this person for that, in this time and not in any other.[12]

Ignatieff's concern (that we are psychologically unable to extend care beyond those whom we know) may be supplemented by a further concern, which is whether care remains a good when applied undiluted to large-scale, political problems. Perhaps our problem is not simply that it is psychologically difficult to care for those who are distant from and unknown to us, but rather that care may be morally transformed when it is extended to such contexts.

This point may be clarified if we concentrate less on the perspective of the carer, and more on the perspective of the recipient of care. The ethics of care draws our attention to qualities which are prominent in dealing with those whom we know and love, and it urges that, via an extension of sympathy, those same qualities may be

extended to unknown others. Thus, we should construe our relationship to (unknown) fellow citizens on the model of our relationship to members of our own family. So expressed, the ethic of care
merely urges an enlargement of the scope of individual sympathy.
However, from the recipient's perspective, the situation may be
rather different: to be the recipient of sympathy from a stranger can
often be offensive and unwelcome. Often, what is desired is not the
compassion of someone better off then ourselves, but rather a recognition of our claims in terms of justice and equality. The substitution
of compassion for justice at the political level was, after all, responsible for some of the most morally disreputable aspects of Victorian
Poor Law, and this should serve as a warning against unbridled
enthusiasm for the extension of care in addressing the problems of
politics in the modern world.

In making this last point, I am not suggesting that compassion
from a stranger can never be welcome or appropriate. Nor am I suggesting that compassion from friends and family is always welcome.
Rather, the point is simply that, on the political level, too much
emphasis on care may serve to disguise the requirements of justice
and equality. Anne Phillips makes a similar point in noting that:

> the contrast between (male) abstraction and (female) specificity is
> running like wildfire through much contemporary feminist
> debate, and if the implication is that the latter is superior to the
> former then I simply do not agree. Compassion cannot substitute
> for the impartiality of justice and equality, for compassion is
> potentially limited to those we can understand – and hence those
> who are more like ourselves. For feminists in particular, this would
> be a risky road to pursue, and it was precisely the demand for
> equality across seemingly impassable barriers of incomprehension
> and difference that gave birth to the feminist tradition.[13]

In the political context, therefore, the language of care presents two
threats: the first is that it will simply result (indeed, has resulted) in
those who present themselves as caring being required to carry the
entire burden of welfare provision. The history of care in the community has been the history of dependence on women, whose role
as carers has substituted for state provision. Thus, in Britain, the 1981
White Paper (*Growing Older*) asserted that:

the primary sources of support and care for elderly people are informal and voluntary. These spring from the personal ties of kinship, friendship and neighbourhood . . . It is the role of public authorities to sustain and, where necessary, develop – but never to displace – such support and care. Care in the community must increasingly mean care *by* the community.[14]

Where the family unit, or the neighbourhood, has been seen as the primary locus of care, women have taken a disproportionate responsibility for the provision of that care, and the situation is unlikely to be improved be feminist adherence to an ethic of care which emphasizes women's 'natural' propensities in this area.

More worrying even than this, however, is the consideration that care is necessarily particularized. It is not mere lack of imagination, but logic (the conceptual problem inherent in legislating care or compassion) which precludes its extension beyond friends and family. Of course, we may well feel compassion for the inhabitants of 'Cardboard City', for the unemployed or for the hungry, but it does not follow that this emotion, on its own, provides the best foundation for political policies of welfare. On the contrary, the development of the modern welfare state was self-consciously a development away from the model of the rich caring for the poor and towards a model of entitlement for all, whether rich or poor. Such a development need not be motivated by scepticism about people's willingness (or ability) to extend care to a wider public. It may also be motivated by the recognition that when care is so extended, it can imply a loss of dignity for the recipient, and a convenient way of disguising the fact that he or she has claims in justice. Put bluntly, the dilemma which faces care theorists is this: if caring is contained within the family, it will tend to lead in the direction of increased insistence that women are the most appropriate carers, but if extended beyond the family to public policy, it will threaten a return to a conception of the welfare state which is based not on entitlement but on charity.

My concern about the ethic of care therefore has two facets: on an individual level, it gives a simplistic and static account of modern identity, one which ignores the conflict and fragmentation inherent in it; and on a wider, political level it renders problematic our response to the needs of strangers. Nevertheless, I believe that an ethic of care does contain important insights which can avoid these difficulties, and I therefore turn now to a proposed reconstruction which, I hope, will indicate the importance of care in moral and political philosophy.

Care and the case of Antigone

In criticizing the language of care as a language appropriate for the political problems of modern society, I urged a distinction between the perspective of those who provide care, and the perspective of those who are the recipients of care. Displaying compassion for unknown others may be seen (by the donor) as merely a matter of enlarging and extending the virtue of sympathy, but receiving compassion from unknown others is often perceived (by the recipient) as morally different from receiving compassion from friends and family. Specifically, when care is institutionalized, it may undermine the claims of justice and present entitlements as mere favours. By concentrating on the perspective of the donor rather than the recipient, therefore, an ethic of care runs the risk of misunderstanding its own central virtue.

More generally, we may wonder whether the ethics of care would acquire a different status if we were to shift attention from the 'active' to the 'passive', and think about care not as something chosen by the carer, but rather as an obligation upon the carer, which is often unchosen, yet remains an obligation. It is this issue which I shall now address.

Earlier in the chapter I made reference to the contrast drawn by Kittay and Meyers between an ethic of care and an ethic of universal reason. They say:

> A morality of rights and abstract reason begins with a moral agent who is separate from others, and who independently elects moral principles to obey. In contrast, a morality of responsibility and care begins with a self who is enmeshed in a network of relations to others and whose moral deliberation aims to maintain these relations.[15]

As we have seen, proponents of an ethic of care then concentrate on the particularities of actual relationships and on the emotions and commitments which sustain them. In other words, they concentrate on the *activity* of the moral agent as one who exhibits qualities of care. However, there is a second insight in the contrast, which often goes unremarked. This is that moral life may be a matter of what is given, just as much as it is a matter of what is chosen. What is characteristic of women's lives is not simply that they give priority to the activity of caring, but also that their traditional role as carers constrains their ability to determine their own lives: as carers, women are frequently victims of their circumstances, rather than creators of their lives. Thus, where a morality of rights emphasizes the individual as *agent* (as one who *elects* moral principles to live by), feminist morality should emphasize the individual as *recipient* (as one who *recognizes* and *accepts* obligations which must be discharged).

The classic example here is Antigone, who is the tragic victim of the conflicting obligations dictated by her roles as sister, daughter and citizen. Sophocles' play is replete with references to these obligations and the effects of their claims upon Antigone. Thus, it begins with the cry 'O sister!', and Antigone goes on immediately to describe 'the death of our two brothers' and how she and Ismene are doomed to suffer 'for our father'. Modern feminists have sometimes interpreted Antigone's situation as one in which familial or domestic considerations take priority over political ones. They understand her tragic choice as a choice of private over public virtue; of care over justice. Thus, Jean Elshtain argues that the play is to be seen as the drama of a woman pitted against 'the arrogant insistencies of statecraft', a defender of 'the domain of women' and 'primordial family morality'.[16] Faced with conflict, Antigone defies the abstract obligations of the state and rejects public life in favour of familial bonds: she rejects the 'male' language of justice in favour of the 'female' language of care. But read in this way, both the tragic nature of the play, and its political dimension, remain unexplained.

Responding to the demand for a political interpretation of Antigone's dilemma, Mary Dietz argues that Elshtain's account is both anachronistic (since the public/private distinction is essentially a liberal construct) and blind to the transformation of private into public which characterises Antigone's action. Dietz says:

> The reason why Antigone is a heroine and Ismene is not has nothing to do with 'private' or 'familial' virtues, for both sisters

loved their brother. The difference between them has to do with political consciousness. Antigone understands that Creon's refusal to allow Polyneices's burial is not just a singular personal insult, but a collective political threat. The former may be countered with a 'modest silence' or supplication; the latter demands decisive political action. Antigone takes such action; Ismene does not.[17]

But neither Dietz nor Elshtain provides a full explanation of the essentially *tragic* nature of Antigone's dilemma. It is not the battle between private and public, nor the transformation of private into public which makes Antigone a tragic heroine. For tragedy, what is required is reference to the inevitability and inescapability of her situation. The references to conflicting roles (sister, daughter, citizen), none of which may voluntarily be renounced, provide the clue to Antigone's tragedy and also, I suggest, to the way in which feminist theory may have application to political practice.

What is of crucial importance to the tragedy of Antigone is the extent to which the roles she occupies are multiple, unchosen and in conflict. She is not simply the champion of domesticity who must suffer for her cause, nor is she merely the translator of private actions into political language. Her role is essentially one which is given rather than chosen – she is the bearer of inconsistent obligations which she neither controls nor chooses, yet which she must honour. Since her obligations conflict, she cannot discharge them all, but since they are all, and equally, obligations, she cannot renounce them without dishonour. Thus, the key moral distinction is not between the family and the polity, nor between the private and the public, but between the chosen and the given. Antigone is characterized by her recognition of the 'givenness' of moral life and of the extent to which it renders us vulnerable to the inconsistent demands of different duties. If we understand feminist ethics as an ethic which emphasizes this, then we will, I believe, be in a position to alleviate the two problems mentioned earlier. We will be able to construct an account of female identity which answers to the complex realities of women's lives, and we will have a more fruitful perspective on the relationship between feminist morality and the claims of politics.

Moreover, this way of interpreting Antigone's situation enables us to distinguish between two distinct objections to an ethic of justice.

We may note that justice is only one value amongst many, and that different kinds of people will give priority to different values. This objection, which has been emphasized by feminists, is powerful but also problematic, for it threatens to create an unbridgeable gulf both between men and women, and between those who are the natural recipients of our care (those who are close to us) and those who are not (those who are distant from us). Unless we can extend care indefinitely, an ethic of care, so understood, will remain unhelpful in dealing with political problems which concern a wider world of unknown others. However, and as we have seen, the indefinite extension of care is both psychologically and conceptually problematic. By contrast, if our objection to an ethic of justice is to its assumption of voluntariness, then we may overcome both these problems. On this account, what is important about the experience of women is not simply that as mothers they care for their children, but also that, as mothers, they are the occupiers of a role. The duties associated with that role constrain women's ability to lead the life of an independent free chooser (they exhibit the incompleteness of an ethic of justice understood as an ethic of choice), and they also conflict with the duties associated with other roles.[18] Moreover, these features of moral life are neither a function of biological determinism nor of social conditioning. They are facts about human life quite generally, but facts which may be more apparent to women, particularly to women who straddle the public/private divide as they attempt to combine the role and status of mother with other roles and aspirations. Emphasis on mothers as the occupiers of roles thus suggests and reflects the unchosen nature of much of moral life. It suggests, with Antigone, that there are responsibilities which are ours 'whether we like it or not', and it suggests that those responsibilities may not always fit very easily together. Connectedly, if we understand an ethic of care as an ethic which emphasizes the 'givenness' of moral life, we may also be better placed to avoid regressive or conservative political conclusions. Earlier I suggested that the assertion of difference, coupled with the implication of moral superiority, may generate an ethic with distinctly elitist political implications. To avoid this, feminist ethics must eschew the language of difference and concentrate instead on the similarities which unite us all. But isn't this to revert to an ethic of justice with all its associated problems of alienation and impersonality? Not necessarily.

An ethic of justice is characterized not simply by the centrality it accords to universality, but also by the emphasis it places on individual autonomy and the role of choice in the selection of moral ends. Feminist theorists have concentrated on the former and, in so doing, have drawn attention to psychological differences between the moral development of men and women. But the latter claim also stands in need of scrutiny. Communitarians, objecting to the prominence of choice in liberal theory, insist that we are 'partly defined by the communities we inhabit', that we are constituted by our attachments to others and by the social context in which those attachments occur. And these societal values and constitutive attachments are almost invariably interpreted as both valuable and benign. Thus Sandel notes that I may owe to others more than justice requires or even permits, 'not by reason of agreements I have made but instead in virtue of those more or less enduring attachments and commitments which taken together partly define the person I am'.[19] By drawing attention to the unchosen roles which we occupy, communitarians hope to exhibit the deficiencies in the liberal conception of the self as autonomous chooser but, so understood, communitarianism lacks a political dimension. The neighbourhoods, homes and communities in which identity is formed are private not public arenas and, as Kukathas and Pettit have pointed out, 'when political questions arise, they often do because of conflicts among these antecedently individuated communities and persons – among these already existing identities'.[20]

Thus, communitarianism recognizes that our social and moral situation is often given rather than chosen, but is silent as to the conflicts which may occur between it and a wider public world. A feminist ethic of care can make good this defect if it responds *both* to liberalism's insistence on choice *and* to communitarianism's neglect of conflict. Again, the experience of mothers may be useful in one of two ways: we may employ it to draw attention to the fact that obligations are not invariably chosen, and we may also employ it to draw attention to the fact that obligations are not always consistent. If feminist ethics simply extols maternal virtues, then it will conspire with communitarianism to exclude women from the political realm.

There are therefore three conditions which feminist ethics must satisfy if it is to have any hope of generating feminist politics. First, it must avoid appeal to women's 'special' or 'different' voice, since the different voice is a domestic voice, and domestic virtues are deformed when they are translated to a public world. Second, and connectedly, it must reject liberal emphasis on the activity of moral life and concentrate instead on the extent to which moral obligations are associated with roles and are unchosen (in this sense, it must ally itself with the communitarian critics of liberalism). Finally, and most importantly, it must distance itself from communitarianism by insisting that the social contexts in which obligations arise are diverse and conflicting. They are the source of pain and, at the limit, of tragedy. Since historically women have often been defined by their social roles, this is a point which they are well placed to make. It is not, however, a point unique to women, but a quite general point about human beings. Indeed, it is an unavoidable consequence of any attempt to move between different communities, and therefore a necessary condition of feminist theory's ability to deliver a practical politics which will do justice to the facts of women's lives.[21]

8
Tragedy, Moral Conflict and Liberalism

The central question of this chapter is how modern liberal political theory can understand and make sense of value pluralism and the conflicts upon which it is premissed. It is a commonplace that liberalism was born out of conflict, and has been partly characterized ever since as a series of attempts to accommodate it within the framework of the nation-state.[1] However, it is also true that liberals have proposed many different routes to the resolution, or containment, of conflict, and these different routes are manifestations of different understandings of conflict itself both within an individual life and between lives. Thus, some assert the irreducible heterogeneity of value: John Stuart Mill famously inveighs against the attempt to model all human life on a single pattern and tells us that 'human beings are not sheep, and even sheep are not indistinguishably alike. A man cannot get a coat or a pair of boots to fit him unless they are either made to his measure or he has a whole warehouseful to choose from; and is it easier to fit him with a life than with a coat?'[2] On Mill's account, plurality is the natural (and indeed desirable) condition of humanity. We should neither hope for nor expect the elimination of conflict, and a world in which there is diversity is richer and better for it.

Others take pluralism to be allied to scepticism: there just are conflicting values, but since we have no justification for deeming any particular way of life 'the best', we must acknowledge conflict as an ineradicable part of the human condition. This latter view does not assert the superiority of a world containing plural values, it merely accepts that where there is a plurality of conflicting values, we will

115

have no basis on which to deem one value preferable or superior to another.

These distinct understandings of the nature of conflict generate distinct responses to its resolution. For the sceptic, conflict is simply a fact, and (often) an unfortunate fact in so far as it generates social and political discord, whereas for the committed pluralist, conflict is, if not itself valuable, at least a necessary concomitant of the heterogeneity of value. The pluralist therefore sees conflict as something inevitable and not wholly regrettable. Probably the most famous modern exponent of this position is Isaiah Berlin, who writes: 'If, as I believe, the ends of men are many, and not all of them in principle compatible with one another, then the possibility of conflict – and of tragedy – can never wholly be eliminated from human life, either personal or social.'[3] Additionally, Berlin argues that the attempt to eliminate conflict is itself one of the most pernicious forces in politics. He inveighs against those who pretend that conflict resolution can be costless and insists that we cannot conceive of a situation in which all value conflict has been eliminated and there has been no loss of value on the way. Moreover, he implies that the elimination of conflict is problematic not only inter-personally but also intra-personally. This, I take it, is the force of his emphasis on the permanent possibility of tragedy at both the personal and the social level.

However, Berlin's emphasis on the dangers of loss inherent in conflict resolution appears to be denied by a rather different characterization of pluralism – one provided by Steven Lukes. In the course of a discussion of the incommensurability of values Lukes writes: 'the very assumption of commensurability would subvert certain values which are what they are in part just because they deny it.' And he goes on to explain this by citing the examples of friendship and family relations, arguing that 'if I were prepared even to consider . . . whether my parental duties can be traded for some greater overall benefit, or against, say, some promise I have made, that might only go to show that I am not a true friend or parent'.[4] On Lukes' account, therefore, pluralism need not generate conflict, for incommensurability implies a refusal to trade off or weigh one value against another. Faced with a choice between familial duty and keeping a promise, the agent ought not even to consider the weight carried by the promise, but should simply act as a good parent.

In order, therefore, for pluralism and incommensurability to generate conflict, something more is required, and this is to be found, I
think, in Alasdair MacIntyre's analysis of the tragic. MacIntyre writes:

> The interest of Sophocles lies in his presentation of a view equally
> difficult for a Platonist or a Weberian to accept. There are indeed
> crucial conflicts, in which different virtues appear as making rival
> and incompatible claims upon us. But our own situation is tragic
> in that we have to recognise the authority of both claims. There
> is an objective moral order, but our perceptions of it are such
> that we cannot bring rival moral truths into complete harmony
> with each other, and yet the acknowledgement of the moral order,
> and of moral truth, makes the kind of question which a Weber
> or a Berlin urges upon us out of the question. For to choose does
> not exempt me from the authority of the claim I choose to go
> against.[5]

The Platonist cannot admit of tragedy because, for him, all value
must ultimately be harmoniously reconcilable. Equally, however,
emphasis on incommensurability is not sufficient for tragedy,
because incommensurability, at least in the form in which Lukes discusses it, denies the conflict which is essential to tragedy. Nor, on
MacIntyre's account, can pluralism of the form advocated by Berlin
fully acknowledge the authority of the value the agent decides
against, and therefore it too denies tragic conflict. For tragic conflict,
therefore, we require both pluralism and a denial of the possibility
of harmonious reconciliation and an acknowledgement that the
value which is decided against has authority. We require pluralism,
plus conflict, plus loss.

In modern liberal political theory, the facts of pluralism, conflict
and loss appear to be acknowledged in high degree. Indeed, and as
has been noted already, modern liberalism begins from these facts
and asks how conflict may nevertheless be accommodated. My
concern in this chapter will be to suggest that, in answering this question, liberals have a tendency to deny the premiss from which they
began. They respond to pluralism, conflict and loss by constructing
a political theory which denies their significance, and hence renders
tragic conflict irrational or incomprehensible. More specifically, they
aspire to 'tame' conflict, first, by insisting that the private should be

subordinated to the public in any conflict between the two, and second, by attempting to substitute principles of justice for the operation of fate. However, and ironically, in so doing, modern liberalism creates the seeds of a new, and essentially modern, tragic situation.

Modern liberalism and the nature of the tragic

I have noted that liberalism was born of the recognition of conflict and that its central aim is to demonstrate ways in which such conflict may be accommodated within the framework of the state. This 'fact' of plurality, and of the conflict attendant upon it, is the starting point of John Rawls's *Political Liberalism*, and in the introduction to that book Rawls declares:

> a modern democratic society is characterized not simply by a pluralism of comprehensive religious, philosophical and moral doctrines, but by a pluralism of incompatible yet reasonable comprehensive doctrines. No one of these doctrines is affirmed by citizens generally. Nor should one expect that, in the forseeable future one of them, or some other reasonable doctrine, will ever be affirmed by all, or nearly all, citizens.[6]

Pluralism, then, is a fact – and not one which can be expected to go away. Since that is so, the task of liberal political theory is to show how the conflict attendant upon it may be channelled and accommodated.

The separation of the political

One very familiar way in which liberalism has attempted to cope with conflict is by insisting upon a separation between the public and the private spheres: within the private realm, individuals may pursue their own conceptions of the good, but in public life those conceptions must be subservient to an overarching conception of the right, or of justice. This distinction between public and private has been extensively criticized, particularly by feminist commentators,

who draw attention to the way in which it characteristically construes the private realm as the realm of the family and thus removes
women, and women's concerns, from the sphere of justice. These
problems are familiar and I shall not dwell on them here, though
I shall refer to them later in the chapter. What I now wish to concentrate on is a slightly different aspect of the public/private distinction, which is the tendency, prevalent in more recent liberal
political philosophy, not merely to distinguish between public and
private, but also to privilege the former over the latter. In *Political
Liberalism* Rawls asserts that under reasonably favourable conditions
that make democracy possible, 'political values normally outweigh
whatever non-political values conflict with them'.[7] The claim is made
yet more starkly by Brian Barry in his book *Justice as Impartiality*.
Commenting on the Irangate controversy, and the question of
whether Oliver North's secretary should have shredded the secret
documents, Barry says: 'the answer is obvious: principles of justice
win . . . to regard loyalty to one's boss as a genuine moral counter-
weight is simply to show a frightening lack of common sense.'[8] And
he seems prepared to generalize this conclusion, arguing that considerations of loyalty, love and commitment to others enter into the
picture only when considerations of justice do not yield a determinate answer. When, however, they do yield a determinate answer
'Justice wins'.

   It is interesting to note that although the claims made by Rawls
and Barry for the priority of justice over loyalty contradict Lukes'
claim, mentioned earlier, they nevertheless result in a similar
problem for those who aspire to accommodate both pluralism and
conflict. Like Lukes, they do not *explain* the conflict which is consequent upon pluralism; rather they *remove* it by establishing a hierarchy of values. Thus, where Lukes insists that a willingness to consider
the relative weight of familial loyalty may bespeak a misunderstanding of it as a value, Barry insists that a willingness to consider
the importance of loyalty bespeaks a 'frightening lack of common
sense'. For Lukes, loyalty must win, else we do not understand what
loyalty is; for Barry, justice must win else we show a frightening lack
of common sense. But the result is the same in both cases: what
begins as an acknowledgement of plurality ends, quite rapidly, in a
denial that plurality generates real conflict.

It is, then, the insistence on a distinction between public and private values, coupled with a priority ordering, which enables modern liberalism to cope with pluralism and the conflict of value attendant upon it. However, this strategy threatens the very premiss on which liberalism itself is initially based, namely that there are values which are irreducibly conflictual and that the conflicts cannot be resolved without loss. To return to the point made by MacIntyre, and quoted earlier, modern liberalism begins by asserting the 'fact' of plurality, and attempting to show how the conflict consequent upon it may be accommodated, but it soon ends by denying conflict altogether, since its insistence on a priority ordering is a covert way of refusing to acknowledge the authority of the claim we choose to go against. Thus, Lukes' argument results in a denial of justice when it is pitted against personal or familial loyalty, and Barry's argument results in a denial of loyalty when it is pitted against justice. Either way, though, the resolution of conflict is purchased at a price – and the price is a genuine recognition of the facts of conflict which motivated liberalism in the first place.

Perhaps none of this would matter were the realm of justice and the realm of personal morality uncontroversially distinct, but notoriously they are not. In a footnote in *Political Liberalism* Rawls discusses the appropriate political response to the problem of abortion. He writes:

> suppose we consider the question in terms of these three political values: the due respect for human life, the ordered reproduction of political society over time, including the family in some form, and finally the equality of women as equal citizens . . . I believe that any reasonable balance of these three views will give a woman a duly qualified right to end her pregnancy during the first trimester . . . any comprehensive doctrine that leads to a balance of political values excluding that duly qualified right [the right to termination] in the first trimester . . . is unreasonable.[9]

This passage is notable both for its (much discussed) insistence that a denial of the right to abortion would be 'unreasonable', and for its (less discussed) assumption that the question falls uncontroversially within the scope of a theory of justice and therefore (presumably) constitutes an example of a case in which private views must be subsumed beneath the requirements of Rawlsian justice. However, and as Simon Caney has pointed out, it is not clear why Rawls believes that there will be no 'fact of reasonable pluralism' about justice and the right.[10] Roman Catholics, who see abortion simply as murder, will be disinclined to interpret their belief either as one which must be dismissed as unreasonable, or as one which should be 'privatized' within a Rawlsian conception of political value. What is much more plausible is that Roman Catholic insistence that abortion should be made illegal is evidence of a different conception of justice. In short, it is evidence of the fact of pluralism about the right.

Caney's point occurs in the context of a discussion of Rawls's requirement of reasonableness, and he suggests that, in at least some places, Rawls adopts the following understanding of reasonableness: 'reasonable persons think that political decisions may not be based upon claims about which intelligent persons disagree.' However, if this is a correct interpretation then, Caney notes, the requirement of reasonableness is far too strong. If consistently applied, it would preclude the state taking any position on abortion, since this is precisely a subject about which intelligent people disagree vigorously. Yet Rawls insists that the state may legitimately take a position on abortion. Additionally, his commitment to the difference principle rests upon a controversial assumption – namely, that the distribution of talents is 'arbitrary from a moral point of view'. However, this assumption, too, is one on which intelligent people can (and do) disagree. Therefore, Caney concludes, if Rawls really means to adopt the strong interpretation of reasonableness, he will find himself precluded from implementing some of the central tenets of his own theory of justice.

Caney is concerned to draw attention to the difficulties inherent in interpreting Rawls's requirement of reasonableness, but his reference to the difference principle may alert us to further problems consequent on Rawls's account. The difference principle flows from the contention that the distribution of talents is arbitrary from a moral point of view, but this claim can be sustained only by insisting upon a particular understanding of the distinction between justice and fate – one which is not wholly implausible, but which is controversial and which, again, has consequences for the understanding of pluralism, conflict and loss inherent in modern liberalism. It is to this I now turn.

Justice and fate

I begin my discussion here, not with a piece of philosophy, but with a quotation from the playwright Arthur Miller:

> There are a thousand things to say about that time [the Depression] but maybe one will be evocative enough. Until 1929 I thought things were pretty solid. Specifically, I thought – like most Americans – that somebody was in charge. I didn't know who it was, but it was probably a businessman, and he was a realist, a no-nonsense fellow, practical, honest, responsible. In 1929 he jumped out of the window. It was bewildering. His banks closed and refused to open again, and I had twelve dollars in one of them. More precisely, I happened to have withdrawn my twelve dollars to buy a racing bike from a friend of mine who was bored with it, and the next day the Bank of the United States closed. I rode by and saw the crowds of people standing at the brass gates. Their money was inside! And they couldn't get it. And they would never get it. As for me, I felt I had the thing licked.
>
> But about a week later I went into the house to get a glass of milk and when I came out my bike was gone. Stolen. It must have taught me a lesson. Nobody could escape that disaster.[11]

The final line, 'nobody could escape that disaster' introduces a pervasive theme in Miller's writing, which is that what, from one perspective, is most naturally represented as a disaster can, from another perspective, be seen only as the deliverance of justice. For Miller, the distinction between justice and fate is, in part at least, agent-relative, and many of his plays take this fact as central. Thus, discussing *Death of a Salesman* he writes:

> To me, the tragedy of Willie Loman is that he gave his life, or sold it, in order to justify the waste of it. It is the tragedy of a man who did believe that he alone was not meeting the qualifications laid down for mankind by those clean-shaven frontiersmen who inhabit the peaks of broadcasting and advertising offices. From those forests of canned goods high up in the sky, he heard the thundering command to succeed as it ricocheted down the newspaper-lined canyons of the city, heard not a human voice,

but a wind of a voice to which no human being can reply in kind except to stare into the mirror at a failure.[12]

We may see Willie Loman as a victim, seduced by the illusions of a corrupt society, but he himself cannot see things that way: he is consumed by the American Dream which dictates that merit is always rewarded by success and that therefore his own failure is a just consequence of his own inadequacies.

The point can and has been generalized. It is an implicit premiss of much modern liberalism that a clear line can be drawn between what counts as an injustice and what counts as a misfortune. Rawls explicitly expresses the expectation that in a just society 'our loves will expose us mainly to the accidents of nature and the contingency of circumstances'.[13] But what we are disposed to attribute to the accidents of nature or contingency of circumstances depends partly on the role we ourselves occupy and partly on the scheme of justice within which we situate ourselves. Thus, many are inclined to construe famine, poverty and unemployment as accidents of nature but, as Judith Shklar has pointed out, the people most likely to do so are those who fear that they may be potentially or actually blameworthy: 'for them, it is a self-protecting move, with a view to similar future events'.[14] Here, the tendency to declare in favour of fortune rather than injustice is a product of one's own place in the wider scheme of things, but it may also be a product of a particular political ideology.

To take a central case in modern political theory, Hayek's 'invisible hand' interpretation of the market results in a clear distinction between fate and justice, but the line between the two is drawn in the place dictated by his understanding of the market as something akin to a force of nature: 'his market is neither fair nor unfair; it knows only winners and losers. It has no will, no purposes, no personality. We cannot hold it responsible for anything at all. Because the market is an impersonal force of nature, those who are injured by it cannot claim that they have suffered an injustice, although many of their normal expectations may have been shattered.'[15]

Both sorts of difficulty are exhibited by Miller's Willie Loman. Willie's moral assessment of his situation is partly a function of his own position in the larger scheme of things and partly a function of his acceptance of a particular political ideology. Thus, the tragic power of the play depends on our ability, as audience, to see what Willie himself cannot see – namely that he has been harshly dealt with. Additionally (and this, I take it, is a central point for Miller) the very fact that we see him as one who has been harshly dealt with, casts doubt upon our willingness to concede that the distinction between justice and fate is clear and uncontroversial. On the contrary, the playwright suggests that the line between the two is value-laden. It is a consequence of specific political commitments, not something which hangs free of them.

All this, of course, arises in the context of a specific tragic play. However, the same point is emphasized in a philosophical context by Bernard Williams, who argues that the ancient Greek understanding of slavery was not, or not most significantly, that it constituted a necessary identity, but that it was a piece of individual bad luck. For the Greeks, he says, being a woman was a necessary identity, but being a slave was a misfortune, even a disaster. Indeed, it was the paradigm case of misfortune, the kind of thing which could befall anyone and which was characterized precisely by its violence and arbitrariness. Williams takes the difference between our understanding of slavery (as a fundamentally unjust institution) and the Greek understanding of slavery (as both socially necessary and personally disastrous) to be indicative of a more general difference in attitude towards the world and our place in it. The Greeks, he claims, did not suppose that because something was necessary it was therefore just, and in this respect their approach to the moral world was more wholesome – less corrupt – than that of much modern liberal political philosophy, which does assume that what is necessary is just, or at least not unjust:

> We, now, have no difficulty in seeing slavery as unjust: we have economic arrangements and a conception of a society of citizens with which slavery is straightforwardly incompatible. This may stir a reflex of self-congratulation, or at least of satisfaction that in some dimensions there is progress. But the main feature of the Greek attitude to slavery was not a morally primitive belief in its justice, but the fact that considerations of justice and injustice were immobilised by the demands of what was seen as social and economic necessity. That phenomenon has not so much been eliminated from modern life as shifted to different places.[16]

The point is reinforced by Shklar, who singles Hayek out as someone who, unusually amongst libertarians, does not blame the poor for their poverty, 'nor does he claim that their situation is not only necessary but also just. It is,' she says, 'much to his credit that he does not yield to the urge to blame the victim.'[17] On the contrary, and for Hayek, the operation of the free market is like a force of nature: its results are unintended and need carry no implication of praise or blame, but the desire to rid the world of such random forces and to deny that we are, any longer, under the thrall of circumstances which are outside our control, is pervasive in much modern liberal political theory. It is also, in large part, commendable, for it militates against a tendency to attribute to fate what is in fact the remediable consequence of political policy.

Nevertheless, there are dangers inherent in supposing that the effects of fate can be completely eliminated or, more particularly, that moving the line between justice and necessity is tantamount to removing it. Just as the ancient Greeks had no idea how to continue their own way of life without perpetuating the institution of slavery, so we now may have no idea how to continue our way of life without permitting continued poverty in the Third World, but it does not follow, and it is not true, that our inability to reconcile these two renders Third World poverty just, any more than the ancient Greeks' inability rendered slavery a just institution. This is the deep point behind Williams' discussion: like the ancients, we find our sense of justice and injustice 'immobilized' by some problems, but unlike them we are inclined not simply to concede our impotence, but to conclude that what has no political remedy cannot be unjust. And this, in the end, is the source of Willie Loman's tragedy – he cannot admit that his own situation is anything other than the deliverance of justice, and via that inability he highlights a way in which modern liberalism not only attempts to substitute justice for fate but, in so doing, gives rise to a new, and distinctively liberal, form of tragedy. For now tragedy arises not from the operation of a cruel and arbitrary fate; it arises from the belief that we can escape fate by extending the power and scope of justice.

In *The Death of Tragedy* George Steiner remarks that 'tragedy is that form of art which requires the intolerable burden of God's presence. It is now dead because His shadow no longer falls on us as it fell on Agamemnon or Macbeth or Athalie'.[18] More generally, we might say that tragedy is impossible in the modern world because we no longer recognize something beyond ourselves: something authoritative and compelling which nevertheless cannot be brought into harmony with our own understanding of the moral order. As we have seen, modern liberalism aspires to 'tame' plurality by the twin strategies of prioritizing the political and rendering us immune to all but the accidents of nature and the contingency of circumstance. What I have suggested, however, is that these strategies are simultaneously untrue and distorting. The distinction between the political and the private is fundamentally unstable, and even if it were not, there is no compelling argument for giving the political priority over the private. On the contrary, the cost of giving priority to the political is that we are forced to neglect rather than accommodate the facts of plurality, conflict and loss.

The second strategy for accommodating conflict also depends upon an unstable distinction – the distinction between justice and fate. I have suggested that what we see as the deliverance of fate is not value-free, but must depend in some part on the wider system of value within which we operate and to which we subscribe. Much liberalism, however, depends upon there being a clear and stable distinction between what is attributable to fate and what is within the domain of justice. Moreover, liberalism often aspires to reduce the scope of fate and substitute justice for it, but in this lie the seeds of a new form of tragedy. Arthur Miller tells us that modern tragedy 'is the consequence of a man's total compulsion to be evaluated justly'. In the context of my argument, I take this to mean two things: tragedy is a consequence of our belief that the world can be rendered fundamentally just, and it is a consequence of our further belief that justice has priority over all other values – that in any conflict between values 'justice wins'. The tragedy of Willie Loman is precisely that he has learned these lessons too well: believing that the race genuinely is to the swift and the battle to the strong, he cannot explain his own failure to himself and therefore he must 'sell his life in order to justify the waste of it'. He is, for these reasons, and somewhat paradoxically, the tragic hero of modern liberal political philosophy.[19]

9
Out of the Doll's House: Reflections on Autonomy and Political Philosophy

Autonomy is, without doubt, one of the most important concepts (maybe *the* most important concept) in modern political philosophy. It holds a central place in John Stuart Mill's *On Liberty*, in John Rawls's *A Theory of Justice* and in Joseph Raz's *The Morality of Freedom.*[1] It is the lodestar of much modern liberalism, and the litmus test by which existing political arrangements are standardly judged. As Brian Barry notes: 'there can be no question but that a conception of the good as autonomy comes with impeccable liberal credentials . . . among contemporary political philosophers of a liberal persuasion, those who do not appeal to justice as impartiality almost all invoke the value of autonomy.'[2] From Kant to Kymlicka and from Rawls to Raz (almost) all agree that autonomy holds a privileged place in modern moral and political philosophy, and (almost) all concur in assigning it centrality in the assessment of political institutions, which are judged, in part, by their ability to promote and foster it. But what exactly is autonomy? Here, agreement runs out and Gerald Dworkin concludes:

> the term is used in an exceedingly broad fashion. It is used sometimes as an equivalent of liberty, sometimes as equivalent to self-rule or sovereignty, sometimes as identical with freedom of the will. It is equated with dignity, integrity, individuality, independence, responsibility and self-knowledge. It is identified with qualities of self-assertion, with critical reflection, with freedom from obligation, with absence of external causation, with knowledge of one's own interests. It is related to actions, to beliefs, to reasons

for acting, to rules, to the will of other persons, to thoughts and to principles. About the only features held constant from one author to another are that autonomy is a feature of persons and that it is a desirable quality to have.[3]

Autonomy, it seems, is a 'catch-all' term, lacking clear definition and deployed primarily for the purposes of evincing approval. Cynically, we might say that nobody knows what it is, but that whatever it is, it is a good thing for individuals to have and for society to promote.

My aims in this chapter are two-fold: first, I want to draw attention to one dominant understanding of autonomy in modern political philosophy; second, I want to question whether autonomy, so understood, deserves the centrality which modern liberal politcal philosophy accords it. My claim will be that it does not and that the dominant understanding overlooks an important set of considerations which cast doubt upon both liberalism's understanding of autonomy and the wisdom of its commitment to it.

First, however, I must say something about what I take autonomy to be. As has already been emphasized, the philosophical literature is replete with diverse and often contradictory accounts. However, one prominent claim, and the one I shall concentrate on here, is that autonomy is a personal ideal according to which individuals are authors of their own lives: to be autonomous is to be able to live out one's plans, projects and aspirations and, in that sense, to 'write the story' of one's own life. The point is most famously made by Isaiah Berlin in his essay 'Two Concepts of Liberty'. Berlin writes: 'I wish my life and my decisions to depend on myself, not on external forces of whatever kind. I wish to be an instrument of my own, not other men's acts of will. I wish to be a subject, not an object . . . I wish to be somebody, not nobody; a doer – deciding, not being decided for.'[4] Similarly, John Stuart Mill notes that: 'If a person possesses any tolerable amount of common sense and experience, his own mode of laying out his existence is the best, not because it is the best in itself, but because it is his own mode.'[5] And Brian Barry identifies autonomy with self-determination, and notes that for advocates of autonomy-based liberalism: 'what is of central importance to human life is that people should make up their own minds about how to live and what to think'.[6] For all these writers, what matters is that people shall be self-determining, they must be the authors of their own lives.

Of course, such authorship can never be complete, nor can it be attained in a social vacuum. Thus, the kinds of stories I can write will always depend, in some part, on the constraints imposed by the circumstances in which I find myself. It is otiose to pretend that there can be such a thing as 'full autonomy' if by that is meant the authorship of one's life independent of all social determinants and divorced utterly from considerations of context. Nevertheless, the ideal is an ideal of partial authorship, and political and social arrangements are to be judged by their degree of conduciveness to that ideal. Social and political arrangements are, we might say, justifiable to the extent that they foster and encourage individual autonomy understood as authorship, and they are suspect to the degree that they obstruct the pursuit of that ideal.

One further caveat: just as the ideal of autonomy need not imply total and unconstrained freedom of choice, so it need not imply a single object of choice. The autonomous agent will not be required to make a single, once for all, decision about how his or her life should go. Autonomy and unity are distinct, and an autonomous agent may (within limits) deploy autonomy in different ways on different occasions. Being autonomous, then, is consistent with having diverse and heterogeneous pursuits.

In brief, autonomy, understood as authorship, is consistent with limitation on choices, and distinct from any requirement that a life shall have a unity. The story of my life will have a setting, and it may well be a story with diverse strands rather than a single 'plot'. It is, nevertheless, an autonomous life to the extent that I am able to mould and fashion it for myself.

In what follows I want to argue that autonomy, so understood, is less important than is commonly believed. By giving centrality to the concept of autonomy as authorship modern political philosophy neglects what is of most significance to many people's lives. In particular, it misrepresents the nature of personal relationships and in consequence advocates social and political arrangements which threaten to distort the realities of individuals' lived experience.

I shall try to substantiate these claims via the examination of a single dramatic case – the case of Nora in Ibsen's *Doll's House*. I take this example partly because it has already attracted considerable philosophical attention and is discussed at some length by Stanley Cavell in his book *Conditions Handsome and Unhandsome*.[7] There, Cavell argues that the case of Nora is the case of a woman trapped in a society which denies her the possibility of autonomy or self-authorship. Nora is denied freedom, and her society is to be condemned for that very reason. Connectedly, (and this is Cavell's central theme), Rawlsian liberal political theory cannot explain that denial of freedom, and that in turn serves to undermine the claims of Rawlsian liberalism to provide a blueprint for a just society. So Cavell takes it for granted that Nora's predicament is correctly characterized as one in which she lacks autonomy, and he also takes it for granted that there is something deeply suspect about any theory which cannot show that that is the case.

By contrast, my claim will be that we should not understand Nora as lacking in autonomy. There is an alternative account of her predicament, one which identifies it as problematic not because she is unable to *write* the story of her own life, but because, and in ways to be explained, she is unable to *read* it. More generally, what makes our lives meaningful and significant is, I shall argue, better explained via an analogy with reading than via an analogy with writing. Given the breadth of the term 'autonomy', it is a moot point whether this conclusion is one which denies the importance of autonomy, or whether it is one which reinterprets its meaning. Either way, though, my claim is that in so far as we understand autonomy on the model of authorship, we run the risk of ignoring important features of what makes life meaningful.

The case of Nora

I begin, then, with the story of *Doll's House*. In Ibsen's play the two central characters are Torvald Helmer and his wife, Nora. Torvald is a successful businessman who, as the play opens, is on the verge of promotion to a high-ranking position in the local bank. This promotion will bring with it wealth and respect from the local community. It represents the culmination of Torvald's ambition. However, success and status have been hard won and during the early years of his marriage to Nora he suffered serious ill health. At that time, and unknown to him, Nora borrowed money to pay for his medical treatment. Because women were not allowed to borrow money without a male guarantor, she forged her father's signature on the official loan documents. As the play progresses it becomes increasingly likely that her misdeed will be discovered, Torvald's career in the bank will be threatened and his reputation as a pillar of the community will be destroyed. In the final scene, Torvald does indeed discover what Nora has done. She hopes that the discovery will make him realize how much she has loved him and how much she has been prepared to do for him. To her horror, he receives the news as proof that he has been married to a forger, a liar and a cheat. His wife is not an innocent and guileless 'doll' he supposed her to be. Rather, she is a common criminal. The final scene of the play focuses on the discussion which ensues, and in which their different and conflicting understandings of their relationship are exposed.

The case of Nora, as the title of the play makes clear, is the case of a woman who is treated as a 'doll', more generally as a child, incapable of making decisions for herself, incapable of understanding, much less handling, financial matters. She is, to all external eyes, a child rather than a woman, in acute need of the protection of a practical man to compensate for her own inadequacies. Not only is this the picture her husband has of her, it is the picture of herself which she projects to the outside world generally, and it is a picture endorsed as appropriate by the society in which she lives. It is a picture which portrays what is 'suitable' for a married woman in a society such as hers. The final, traumatic scene in which Nora realizes that this is the picture endorsed by her husband and her society is the focus of most critical discussion and of Cavell's analysis of the play. I turn now to that analysis.

Cavell's analysis

Cavell's aim in discussing *Doll's House* is to draw attention to what he perceives to be defects or limitations in modern liberalism generally, and especially in the liberalism of John Rawls. As has been noted already, many forms of liberalism are premised on the assumption that people are, essentially, autonomous agents, and that a political order is to be judged by its ability to foster that autonomy. It is Cavell's claim that Rawls's political theory ultimately denies individual autonomy to some citizens, and that *Doll's House* provides an example of the way in which it does that.

Briefly, Cavell's argument is as follows: beginning with the belief that people are autonomous agents, liberal political theory emphasizes the importance of consent in the construction of social and political institutions generally and of the rules of justice in particular. The autonomy of individuals is, we might say, acknowledged by allowing them a voice in the determination of the rules which are to govern their society. The contractual model, then, is one which recognizes the importance of people being at least part authors of their own lives, and it does that precisely by allowing them to determine the rules under which they are to live. Social institutions are just if they are such that autonomous agents could and would agree to them. However, as a woman, Nora has had no voice in this 'initial conversation' which determines the rules of justice which prevail in her society. In this respect, she has been denied autonomy.

Additionally, and yet more worryingly, once the rules have been determined by the initial conversation their status is, says Cavell, analogous to the rules of a game. Just as what counts as being out in a game of baseball is determined by the rules governing baseball, so what counts as unjust is determined by the agreed rules of justice, and it is no more legitimate to claim (in Nora's case), 'I forged a document but did not behave morally badly' than it is to say (in the case of a game), 'I broke the rule but am not out'. Yet the former is precisely what Nora *does* want to say. She believes that, although she has broken the rules of the society, she has not acted morally wrongly. She has forged a document, but in so doing she has acted morally well. As Cavell understands it, Rawls's account precludes this response from Nora and, at that level too, it denies her a voice.

For Cavell, then, there are two distinct ways in which Rawls's theory denies Nora's autonomy (where autonomy is understood as authorship). First, it denies her a voice in the initial conversation which determines the rules of justice for the society. Second, it denies her the language with which to express her disagreement with those rules once they have been decided upon. As Mulhall puts it (glossing Cavell):

> she has been deprived of freedom, of having a say in the constitution of her society. As a result, that society does not give expression to a further reach of her autonomous personality but rather cripples and distorts it, forcing her into conformity with

the voices of others, depriving her of a part in the conversation of justice and so depriving her of her own real, enacted existence as a citizen.[8]

There are, of course, important questions here about Cavell's interpretation of Rawls's theory. In particular, his interpretation of Rawls's analogy between the rules of a game and the rules of justice is highly contentious. However, what I wish to concentrate on are not matters of textual interpretation, but the quite general assumption that a theory which denies individual autonomy is suspect, together with the connected assumption that autonomy is a matter of authorship. Cavell appears to take it for granted that autonomy is to be understood in that way, and he also seems to take it for granted that it is a serious criticism of any form of liberalism (including Rawlsian liberalism) that it denies such authorship. It is these assumptions which I wish to question and it is also part of my aim to provide an alternative model of what makes life valuable – one which depends much less heavily on autonomy understood as authorship.

An alternative account

In *After Virtue* Alasdair MacIntyre writes:

> man is in his actions and practice, as well as in his fictions, essentially a story-telling animal. He is not essentially, but becomes through his history, a teller of stories that aspire to truth. But the key question for men is not about their own authorship; I can only answer the question 'What am I to do?' if I can answer the prior question 'Of what story or stories do I find myself a part?'[9]

In what follows I want to take MacIntyre's central claim (that I can only answer the question 'What am I to do?' if I can answer the prior question 'Of what story or stories do I find myself a part?') and apply it to the case of Nora. *Pace* Cavell, I shall argue that Nora's predicament is not essentially that of a woman who is unable to *write* the story of her life. Rather, it is the predicament of a woman who has systematically *misread* the story of her life. More generally, and following MacIntyre, I shall argue that successful reading is primary and successful writing only secondary. To that extent, modern emphasis on autonomy as authorship is partial and potentially distorting of our understanding of what makes life valuable and what makes political and social institutions legitimate.

What then is involved in interpreting Nora as an unsuccessful reader rather than an unsuccessful writer? It is to this question that I now turn and, following Cavell, I shall concentrate on the final scene of the play – the scene in which Torvald discovers what it is that Nora has done.

Re-reading Nora

There are three distinct dimensions through which we might trace Nora's misreading of her situation: first, she misreads the relationship between the laws of society and personal attachments. In other words, she misreads the world in which she finds herself. Second, and connectedly, she misreads her relationship with Torvald. Finally, she misreads herself. In the last act of the play these three kinds of misreading are exposed both to the audience and to Nora herself. They serve, moreover, to highlight the personal and political costs attached to according high priority to autonomy understood as authorship. In this section I shall explain each of these misreadings, and in the following (and final) section I shall try to say something about their consequences for our understanding of autonomy.

Nora's misreading of her society is seen in her astonishment that the law can forbid an act which is undertaken from love. Although she knows that she has broken the law in forging her father's signature, she nevertheless believes that her act is justifiable because it was done to help her sick husband and her dying father. She believes that this motivation, the motivation of personal loyalty and love, is one which should override legal considerations, and she protests: 'Now I find that the law is quite different from what I thought, and I simply can't convince myself that the law is right. That a woman shouldn't have the right to spare her old father on his death-bed, or to save her husband's life! I can't believe things like that.' Although, of course, Nora understands that she has acted illegally, she cannot believe that she has acted morally badly. If the law says she has, then the law is wrong. Here, then, we have a sense in which Nora misreads the world. She is mistaken about the status of the laws relative to personal loyalties, and when she discovers what that status is, she is appalled.

Moreover, her misreading of the world in which she lives brings with it a misreading of her relationship with Torvald and indeed a misreading of Torvald himself. For her discovery that the law stands above (or takes priority over) personal relationships is also a discovery that *for Torvald* the law stands above personal relationships. Thus, when faced with a choice between obedience to the law and loyalty to Nora, he chooses to obey the law. He says, 'Nora, I'd gladly work night and day for you, and endure poverty and sorrow for your sake. But no man would sacrifice his *honour* for the one he loves.' To which she replies, 'Thousands of women have.' Not only has Nora been mistaken about the relative priority of law and personal attachment in the eyes of society, she has also been mistaken about their relative priority in Torvald's eyes and, as a consequence, she has been mistaken about Torvald himself. She had imagined that he would sacrifice everything, including honour, for her, as she would sacrifice everything for him. In this she is wrong, and her mistake now leads her to conclude that she has been married to a stranger (the word 'stranger' is repeated several times in the final scene and has a significance which I shall discuss in the final section of the chapter).

Third, and most poignantly, the final scene is one in which Nora is brought to a realization that she has misread herself. As we have seen, her misreading of the relationship which holds between law and personal attachment brings with it a misreading of the relationship which holds between herself and Torvald (he is not willing to sacrifice everything for her, as she is for him), and also a misreading of Torvald himself (he is exposed as a man who cares more about his appearance in the eyes of the world than about his own wife). It follows from all this that Nora's own life, her hopes, her plans, her aspirations and her actions, have been based on a deceit, and she concludes that she has, in fact, never been happy: 'I thought I had, but really I have never been happy.'[10]

This final remark reveals the extent to which Nora's predicament is more a function of her misreading of the world and her place in it, than it is a function of her inability to write the story of her life. In fact, though in a rather ironical sense, she *has* written the story of her life. She has attained the things she set out to attain – has helped her husband, brought up her children, earned money to maintain the family home and in general 'moulded' her life. But, *pace* Cavell, her situation remains tragic, not because she has been denied autonomy, but rather because she has exercised autonomy in a world which she has systematically misunderstood.

Consequences of the interpretation

What consequences follow from this interpretation of Nora as unsuccessful reader rather than unsuccessful author of her life? In this final section I want to gesture towards some consequences which might follow both for political philosophy and for our more general understanding of what makes a life valuable for the person who leads it. Following the earlier division, I shall first say something about the consequences of Nora's misreading of the relationship between law and personal commitment, then I shall discuss the consequences of her misreading of Torvald, and finally I shall discuss the ways in which these two considerations might inform our assessment of a political theory grounded in a conception of autonomy as authorship.

In *Notes for the Tragedy of Modern Times* Ibsen writes:

> There are two kinds of moral law, two kinds of conscience, one in man and a completely different one in woman. They do not understand each other; but in matters of practical living the woman is judged by man's law, as if she were not a woman but a man.[11]

These remarks suggest a feminist interpretation of Ibsen's play. They suggest that, like many modern feminist writers, Ibsen sees women as more responsive than men to the demands of particular others. Indeed, there is an obvious parallel to be drawn between Ibsen's remarks and Carole Gilligan's claim that in moral matters men and women speak 'in a different voice'. Women are more attentive to the needs of others, more concerned with responsibilities and relationships, less concerned with rights and rules. The now familiar distinction between an ethic of justice and an ethic of care thus fits smoothly with Nora's rejection of the priority which Torvald gives to legal considerations and with her bewilderment at his willingness to sacrifice their marital relationship at its altar. So we might read the play as having a distinctively feminist theme – one which, in the modern parlance, urges the priority of care over justice.

However, this is not the only lesson to be learned from the play, which also provides us with considerations which pull in a rather different direction, and which are more salient to our examination of autonomy as authorship. Critics of the ethic of care often protest that the injunction to care is one which carries with it an implicit invitation to renounce one's autonomy. Care for others, it is said, can all too rapidly become chronic self-denial. It can threaten women's autonomy and render them liable to become victims of the incessant demands made on them by others. Yet ironically, the final scene of *Doll's House* is one in which it is Torvald, not Nora, who is seen to be lacking in autonomy. By refusing to give up his 'honour' for her he not only indicates that she matters less to him than the impersonal laws of his society (his is the ethic of justice, hers is the ethic of care), he also indicates that it is he who is prey to the opinions of others. Nora insists on making her own decisions about 'which is right – the world or myself', and in this she contrasts starkly with Torvald for whom there is no questioning of the world, but only a submissive acceptance of it and its values. Somewhat paradoxically, then, it is Nora's very adherence to an ethic of care (her insistence on placing personal loyalty above the demands of impartial justice) which in one sense gives evidence of her autonomy. Unlike Torvald, she is not driven by the laws of the society in which she finds herself, but is able to decide what is right for herself. In deciding for her family and against the rules of society, she expresses the priority which personal commitments have for her and also gives assurance that she is, in some sense, the author of her own life.

However, it is important to understand the precise sense in which she is the author of her life, for Nora does not exhibit the simple form of autonomy as authorship implied by Berlin: 'I wish my life and my decisions to depend on myself, not on external forces of whatever kind. I wish to be an instrument of my own, not others' acts of will.' Berlin's account implies a stark distinction between self and others. *My* projects and *my* decisions are to be distinguished from the projects and decisions of other people, and while other people might contribute to those projects, it is none the less *my* projects to which they will be contributing. Conversely, of course, other people can constitute a threat to the pursuit of my projects, and indeed a large part of the emphasis on autonomy as authorship is motivated precisely by a recognition of that danger.

What Nora's case shows is that this distinction between self and others is often untrue to the realities of our personal lives. Nora does not construe her projects and decisions as distinct from those of her husband and family. On the contrary, the two are intimately inter-twined for her, and her own well-being is inextricably linked with their well-being. At the personal level, therefore, the distinction between self and others is partial and distorting because it neglects those relationships (relationships of love and friendship) which are constitutive of who I am. Thus, a mother will not characteristically see her own aims and projects as distinct and separable from those of her children. Similarly, people who are married will see their pro-jects as *theirs* collectively – not as individually 'his' and 'hers'. By neglecting this fact, the proponent of autonomy as authorship dis-torts what is valuable in our lives and simultaneously distorts the relationships which we have with others.

Moreover, this point has implications for political philosophy. Implications which are emphasized by Michael Sandel when he notes that a society premised on the value of autonomy as authorship will be, at root, a society of strangers – a society which will have diffi-culty accommodating those constitutive relationships which define what we are and which acknowledge the ways in which our own pro-jects may be inextricably linked with those of others.[12]

Thus, when Nora refers to Torvald as a stranger, there are two ways in which her statement can be interpreted. He is a stranger because he is not what she has always believed him to be. He rejects the values which she believed were central to both their lives. And he is also a stranger because, by giving priority to the law over personal loyalty, he indicates that the demands of strangers (law-makers) are more important than his attachments to his own wife. Faced with a choice between the impersonal laws of society and the needs of his wife, Torvald chooses law and thus, in a quite literal sense, 'estranges' Nora.

There are, I think, three very general conclusions to be drawn from these considerations. First, if we aspire to encourage and develop autonomy, then we must be aware that autonomy is not properly understood simply as an individual ideal. It is also an ideal which has implications for the ways in which we relate to others. When understood as authorship, autonomy carries with it the implication that our plans and projects are clearly distinguishable from the plans and projects of others and, as the case of Nora makes plain, this is untrue of many of the most important plans and projects in our lives.

It follows that the ideal of autonomy cannot be one which merely enables each person to live whatever life he or she chooses – to be self-determining. Such a conception of autonomy is not simply untrue to the reality of our lives, it also (and thereby) threatens to provide a distorted understanding of those constitutive relationships which define who we are. Indeed, it is exactly this deformation of which Torvald shows himself to be the victim when he gives the law priority over Nora, and more generally, it is this deformation which is implicit in the demands made by a political philosophy premissed on autonomy understood as authorship.

Finally, and most importantly, the discussion of *Doll's House* illuminates the fact that autonomy presupposes a background of values, and where an individual misunderstands that background, it is not simply that she is damaged by being denied autonomy. Rather, she is mocked because her life is based on a deception. Nora largely succeeds in writing the story of her life, but in spite of that fact (or perhaps even because of it) she is a tragic figure, and her tragedy lies in the very fact that her autonomy has been exercised in a political and personal world which she has systematically misunderstood. Therefore, if we are to write the story of our lives, we must first read the context of our lives. As MacIntyre insists, we can only answer the question 'what am I to do?' If we can answer the prior question 'of what story or stories do I find myself a part?' To which I would add: 'And we must read our own stories accurately.'[13]

10
Strangers in Paradise: the Unhappy Marriage of Feminism and Conservatism

> You wanted a woman's culture. Well, now there is one. It isn't what you meant, but it exists. Be thankful for small mercies.[1]

The quotation, taken from Margaret Atwood's novel, *The Handmaid's Tale*, expresses an anxiety about the way in which the demands of feminist radicalism may issue in moral and political conservatism. Atwood's novel is set in a future North American society, Gilead, where, as a result of nuclear accidents and AIDS, the population is seriously depleted, most survivors are sterile and the future of the human race is threatened. In this society women, particularly women of child-bearing age, are rare and valuable commodities. They are protected from all forms of sexual assault, harassment and violence; pornography is banned and the streets are safe for women to walk in. Many of the legal demands of 1970s feminists have been satisfied, but the resulting society is not a feminist utopia; it is a dystopia whose origin Atwood traces not simply to natural and scientific disaster, but also to the combined effects of earlier moral conservatism and feminist radicalism. The narrator, Offred, looks back on the earlier society (North America in the mid-1980s) and recalls her mother's 'pure' feminism, her involvement in anti-pornography book burnings and Reclaim the Night marches. She reflects on her mother's political aims and concludes; 'you wanted a woman's culture. Well, now there is one. It isn't what you meant, but it exists. Be thankful for small mercies.' In Gilead, radical feminism and conservative moralism have united to deliver a feminist dystopia in which the protection of women is a cloak for oppression and sexual safety is purchased at the price of personal liberty. Moreover, and like most dystopian writing, *The Handmaid's Tale* is not merely a description of what could happen at some time in the future; it is in part a commentary on what is already happening in the western world of the late twentieth century.

This chapter takes its cue from Atwood's anxiety. There are a number of contemporary political issues on which feminists (particularly radical feminists) have combined forces with moral conservatives in an attempt to change legislation. The most obvious example is in the debate about pornography, but there are also alliances between feminism and conservatism in debates about reproductive technology, surrogacy and speech codes. Nor are these alliances entirely new. In the nineteenth century, feminists in both Britain and America joined forces with moral conservatives in an attempt to gain support for the suffrage campaign, and although such coalitions are often excused as strategic ploys, they are by now too familiar and too frequent to be dismissed quite so lightly. The claim that in political activism we must take whatever friends we can find is undermined if our friends too often turn out to be of a particular political complexion.

Moreover, there is a troubling irony in this particular friendship, for moral conservatism has historically been associated with the oppression, not the liberation of women. It has a clear and distinct understanding of the good and is disposed to impose that understanding on others in a way which is inimical to toleration. This raises the possibility that feminism too is fundamentally intolerant: once the poachers have turned gamekeeper, there is a danger that they will promulgate their conception of the good in disregard of others and thus, as one writer has put it, 'the circle between left and right will finally be closed'.[2]

My aims in this chapter are first to substantiate the claim that the political alliances between feminism and conservatism are more than unhappy coincidence; second, to identify some of the causes of those alliances; and finally to indicate ways in which feminism might avoid some of the graver dangers of association with moral conservatism. This last aim is particularly important, and not only for strategic reasons: Atwood's novel shows clearly how feminist aspirations may be subverted by the political ideals of moral conservatism. It is also important because there is, to my mind, something peculiarly unappetizing about intolerance displayed by a group which itself claims to be (or have been) oppressed. This is not, of course, to suggest that absolutely everything can or should be tolerated, either now or in a future feminist utopia. It is merely to note that in so far as feminists are concerned about oppression, they should be particularly worried if their (our) own political proposals turn out to have potentially intolerant political implications.

The closing circle

Alliances, or suspected alliances, between feminists and moral conservatives are many in number. Indeed, they go back to the origins of feminism itself, although it is frequently argued that they constitute no more than marriages of political convenience. The most obvious alliance is in the nineteenth-century campaign against the Contagious Diseases Acts which was instrumental in the birth of the suffrage movement. The Contagious Diseases Acts, which were passed in Britain in 1864, 1866 and 1869, provided for the periodic genital examination of garrison town prostitutes, and their rationale was to protect soldiers from sexually transmitted diseases. Feminist objections to the Acts focused on the double standard of sexual morality which was implicit in them, for while the spread of sexually transmitted disease was undoubtedly a matter of grave social concern, the solution to the problem was not thought to lie in the control of male sexuality. Rather, provision must be made for the safe satisfaction of male 'needs'. Thus, women suspected of being 'common prostitutes' could be arrested and registered as such. If found to be infected, they could be detained for up to nine months, and imprisoned should they fail to cooperate.

The history of the campaign against the Contagious Diseases Acts is complex and confused, but one thing which is clear is that as it gathered momentum over a period of some twenty years, a rift developed between two kinds of feminist: those who were specifically concerned with the injustice and hypocrisy of the Acts themselves, and those who had a larger moral agenda. One historian has argued that this rift may be clearly discerned in the relationship between the leaders of the LNA (The Ladies National Association for the Repeal of the Contagious Diseases Acts) and its grass-roots members, for while the former stressed the importance of political agitation, the latter highlighted religious objections to regulation and were to 'prove susceptible to the more repressive purity crusades of the 1880s'.[3] These crusades, carried on through organizations such as the National Vigilance Association, promulgated the belief that legislation could and should be used to 'force people to be moral' and even the LNA itself, under the leadership of Josephine Butler, developed into a broad social purity alliance, not easily distinguishable from 'moral repressionists' who called for the prohibition of indecent advertising, penalties for male homosexuality and the commital of the children of prostitutes to industrial schools. As Christine Bolt concludes:

> The overall benefits to the British women's movement of female participation in social purity campaigns were clearly mixed . . . the emphasis of some of the campaigns was on women's duties, not their rights; on desexualising and restricting women, not freeing them to work out an independent vision of female sexuality. They associated feminists with puritanism while making them some very powerful male enemies.[4]

Moreover, the association between feminism and moralism survived the repeal of the Contagious Diseases Acts and was influential in the suffrage campaign in both Britain and America, where liberal insistence on the equality of men and women was often accompanied by arguments based on women's superior moral status. Thus, the American feminist, Carrie Chapman Catt, asked:

> Do you know that extending the suffrage to women increases the moral vote; that in all states and countries that have adopted suffrage the vote of disreputable women is practically negligible, the slum wards of cities invariably having the lightest women vote and the respectable residence wards the heaviest; that only one out of every twenty criminals are women; that women constitute a minority of drunkards and petty misdemeanants; that for every prostitute there are at least two men responsible for her immorality; that in all the factors that tend to handicap the progress of society, women form a minority, whereas in churches, schools and

all organizations working for the uplift of humanity, women are a majority?[5]

But if the deployment of these moral arguments is not in doubt, their status is certainly contentious, and many feminists now claim that the appearance of conservatism is deceptive. Nineteenth-century feminists urgently desired political and legal change. In order to attain this, they needed to mobilize as many people as possible in support of their cause, and the political realities in both Britain and America were such that arguments from moral purity were the ones most likely to gain widespread and popular support. Thus, Katzenstein and Laitin argue that:

> it was the incorporation of 'the morality of caring' into the suffrage claim that helped to turn the movement from its limited size at the turn of the century into a mass effort. Like temperance campaigns that had always drawn numbers far in excess of the suffrage movement in the latter half of the century, the social housekeeping phase of the suffragist movement was able to attract women into the campaign who otherwise might have found suffrage threatening their attachment to the family.[6]

The assumption here is that appeal to women's superior moral status was pragmatic rather than principled. It was a necessary precondition of attaining the desired legal and political reforms and, as such, a permissible strategic device for nineteenth-century feminists.

However, alliances between feminism and moral conservatism have survived the demise of the suffrage campaign and, in recent years, have surfaced again in a number of contexts. These include the debates about reproductive technology, about surrogacy, about speech codes on university campuses and, most notably, about pornography. In their attempts to change the anti-pornography laws of the United States, Andrea Dworkin and Catherine MacKinnon have accepted assistance from moral conservatives, and it is reported that MacKinnon defended this strategy by arguing that 'if someone is willing to stand on your side you don't throw them out'.[7] Here, history repeats itself and, as with nineteenth-century feminism, so too in the late twentieth century, central political campaigns threaten to create a rift within the feminist movement. Katie Roiphe's controversial book, *The Morning After*, accuses MacKinnon of a new form of moralism, and Roiphe writes:

> When the antipornographic imagination meets feminism, what comes out is a moral universe, although MacKinnon denies it. What comes out is a universe of victims and aggressors, of viola- tion, subjugation, dominance, and oppression . . . MacKinnon's well-articulated universe is divided into bold stripes of good and evil. The force is with her, but the force of what? The force is the conservative social atmosphere, and conservative political figures. The force is religious censors, and the force is social fear. In the midst of a confusing, conservative time, she is offering a straight- forward conservative message.[8]

Here again, the charge against feminism is that, by allying itself with moral conservatism, it creates and sustains a picture of women as helpless, passive, and subjugated – the impotent victims of uncon- trolled, and largely uncontrollable, male sexuality. The ghost of Carrie Chapman Catt stalks: 'for every prostitute there are at least two men responsible for her immorality.'

Additionally, both nineteenth- and late twentieth-century femi- nism of this kind confer on women a special, 'moral' voice: women are not merely passive, but morally superior to men. Nineteenth- century repealers thought it women's function to 'form public opinion by their moral influence' and similarly the supporters of the Dworkin–MacKinnon ordinance have invoked the morality of care in defence of their position: 'the model antipornography ordinances, which are written in the language of rights, sound strained and unconvincing in their constitutional appeals. Without the counter- part moral message, these ordinances would ring hollow.'[9]

These considerations suggest that the periodic alliances between feminism and moral conservatism are more than merely coinci- dental, for beneath the common political project lies a common conception of woman's nature, and a common moral vision. Both nineteenth- and twentieth-century 'repealers' invoke images of women as sexually pure or sexually passive, and both go on to insist that that purity must be preserved by restricting the activities of men. In the case of the nineteenth-century repealers, this took the form of a call for 'respectability' on the part of women and sexual self-restraint on the part of men. In the case of twentieth-century anti-pornography campaigners, it again invokes the moral superiority of women (women's 'different voice'), and seeks legal redress in the restraint of male sexuality rather than an assertion of female sexuality. Thus, both arguments spring from a specific conception of the morally good, and result in a demand for the promulgation of that good via the use of law. Law becomes the primary tool whereby people (particularly men) may be 'forced to be moral'.

In recent years much attention has been paid to the 'worrisome' connections between feminist and conservative arguments against pornography, and many causes of the alliance have been suggested. Connectedly, there has been much feminist interest in the communitarianism of writers such as Alasdair MacIntyre and Michael Sandel, whose rejection of the atomism of liberal political theory has been highly praised by many feminists. This philosophical discussion also serves to reinforce the resonance between feminism and conservatism, though this time at the level of philosophical theory rather than of political practice. I shall return to this point later. For now, however, I wish to concentrate on a feature of the debate which has, I believe, gone unremarked. This is that feminist political activism of the kind exemplified by the two campaigns mentioned above, is a manifestation of a certain, rather traditional, kind of utopian thinking. In utopian writing, it is contrasted with critical utopian thinking, and in Michael Walzer's book *Exodus and Revolution*, it is referred to as 'messianic' thinking. In what follows I shall attempt to explain what I mean by these terms, and to show how feminist repealers have succumbed to this kind of thinking. Additionally, I shall suggest ways in which an appeal to critical rather than traditional utopian thinking, or to exodus rather than messianic politics, might serve to distance feminism from the kinds of moral conservatism with which it has been allied since the earliest days of feminist activism.

Exodus and critique

In *Exodus and Revolution* Walzer writes:

Since late medieval or early modern times, there has existed in the West a characteristic way of thinking about political change, a pattern that we commonly impose upon events, a story that we repeat to one another. The story has roughly this form: oppression, liberation, social contract, political struggle, new society. We call the whole process *revolutionary*, though the events don't make a circle unless oppression is brought back at the end; intentionally, at least, they have a strong forward movement.[10]

He shows how this form of thinking has its roots in the biblical story of the Exodus: the delivery of the children of Israel from Egypt into the Promised Land provides a model for stories of political struggle throughout the western world and has been invoked by figures as diverse as Cromwell, Robert Owen, Ernst Bloch and Martin Luther King. Of course, and as Walzer notes, this model is not universal, nor is its meaning transparent:

within the frame of the Exodus story one can plausibly emphasize the mighty arm of God or the slow march of the people, the land of milk and honey or the holy nation, the purging of the counter-revolutionaries or the schooling of the new generation. One can describe Egyptian bondage in terms of corruption or tyranny or exploitation. One can defend the authority of the Levites or of the tribal elders or of the rulers of tens and fifties. I would only suggest that these alternatives are themselves paradigmatic; they are *our* alternatives. In other cultures, men and women read other books, tell different stories, confront different choices.[11]

Crucially, however, the alternatives which the Exodus story presents are between an emphasis on the journey (the long, slow march) and an emphasis on the end (the Promised Land). The story of the Exodus is both a story about a promised future, a destination, and a story about the journey which a people must make in order to arrive at that destination. And the version of the story which emphasizes the journey has different political implications from the version which emphasizes the destination. Walzer refers to the former as Exodus politics and to the latter as messianic politics, but a similar distinction is to be found in the contrast between traditional and critical utopian writing: traditional utopian writing emphasizes the end point (the perfect society), whereas critical utopian writing emphasizes the transition from original to utopian society. Thus, 'in critical utopian thinking, utopia is not simply a *place*, it is a *practice*, the utopian place does not passively stand as an alternative to the present, it becomes part of the overall movement to change that world'.[12]

Moreover, stories which emphasize the journey rather than the destination are more alert to the ways in which the character of the people themselves will change during the journey: Exodus politics and critical utopian thinking, unlike messianic politics or traditional utopian thinking, tell how the people are transformed in their search for the Promised Land, and it follows that the Promised Land, when finally it is realized, is rather different from, and less perfect than, the land which was originally promised. This is in part because, as Walzer puts it, 'the land would never be all it could be until its new inhabitants were all that they should be'.[13] The promise is relational, and its fulfilment depends upon the consciousness and moral character of the people as much as on the character of the world.

Here, then, are three features of Exodus or critical utopian thinking which distinguish it from messianic or traditional utopian thinking: it emphasizes the journey, not the destination; it draws attention to the ways in which the people will change in the making of the journey; and it insists that there will be an interdependence between the Promised Land and the people who inhabit it. By contrast, traditional utopian thinking and messianic politics concentrate on the destination, the land flowing with milk and honey. They remain silent about the need for any change in the people who journey to the promised land, and do not see the utopian society as a function of the character of the people who inhabit it. The promised land is literally 'given' to a people who remain largely the same at the end of their journey as they were at the beginning.

The gift outright

What I want to suggest is that alliances between feminism and conservatism arise when the aspirations of feminist politics take a traditional rather than a critical utopian turn – when they are informed by messianic rather than Exodus thinking. If this is so, then the way forward for feminist politics may be to remain within the tradition of revolutionary thinking which Walzer characterizes as 'our' way of thinking, but to be clear that the direction for that thinking should indeed be critical, not traditional; it should invoke Exodus and not messianic politics. In brute practical terms, this will involve making a sharp distinction between forms of feminism which draw attention to the inadequacy of existing law, and forms of feminism which subscribe to a larger moral agenda, particularly an agenda which assumes the moral superiority of women. I shall argue that once feminism invokes this larger moral agenda, it is ineluctably drawn into practices of intolerance which simultaneously keep women in a state of oppression and condone the oppression of others. It results, not in a feminist utopia, but in Gilead.

The pattern of thinking which Walzer characterizes as revolutionary – oppression, liberation, contract, political struggle, new society – is a pattern regularly appealed to by feminist activists and feminist theorists alike and I shall say no more about it here, but simply assume that this story is the one most often told by feminists themselves. Indeed, feminism is often defined as any theory which sees the relationship between the sexes as one of inequality, subordination or oppression and which aims to identify and remedy the sources of that oppression. However, and as has been suggested above, within this pattern of revolutionary thinking, there may be either an emphasis on the journey or an emphasis on the destination, and that in turn affects the importance placed on the character of the people, and the relationship between them and the utopian society or promised land. Crucially, however, the distinction between Exodus and messianic thinking turns on whether deliverance from oppression is believed to involve changes in the people themselves, or whether it involves simply a change in the circumstances in which they find themselves. Are the oppressed people deemed to be morally pure, or do they themselves stand in need of moral transformation?

This question returns us to the debate between communitarianism and liberalism which was referred to earlier in the chapter, for it draws attention to a problem about the way in which we characterize the relationship between people and the world in which they find themselves. Of course, no one will deny that there must be some connection between people and their social situation, but the quarrel between liberalism and communitarianism is often understood as precisely a quarrel about what that relationship is. For liberals, it is argued, the individual must strive to rise above his social situation and decide what he wants to be independent of it. By contrast, and for communitarians, what one is is determined in large part by one's social setting. But if this is so, then there is a serious question about how we can attain any critical distance from our social setting and how we can criticize it effectively – or at all. The consequences of this for feminism are spelled out by Elizabeth Frazer and Nicola Lacey: 'if the basic communitarian claim is that moral and political argument is validated within particular cultural discourses and practices, whose role in constructing human identity must be recognised, it is difficult to see how one is to attain the critical capacity to judge the sexism, patriarchy or any other feature of the culture in question'.[14] The conservatism implicit in communitarianism is thus traced to the emphasis it places on the close connection between our own identity and the world in which we live.

This is an interesting and, in this context, slightly puzzling turn of events. Communitarianism drives in the direction of conservatism because it places *too much* emphasis on the connection between individual identity and social situation, but messianic thinking also drives in the direction of conservatism because it pays *too little* attention to the relationship between individual identity and social situation. Put differently, the problem with communitarianism is that it threatens to condone practices such as sexual harassment, interpreting it as courtesy, flattery or chivalry. In so far as these are features of a specific culture they are, for communitarians, difficult to criticize. Communitarianism accepts as given, and as self-validating, the moral practices of existing societies, but in a perverse way, messianic thinking also accepts the moral practices of existing societies, since its conception of utopia is one which neglects the extent to which the characteristics and qualities of the liberated people are themselves a function of their previously oppressed state. To give a specific example, both the moral purity faction of the LNA and the radical feminists in the anti-pornography campaign, laud precisely those qualities in women which are held to be consequent upon their oppression in patriarchal society. If the complaint against patriarchal societies is that they legitimize a view of women as sexually passive by, for example, construing as chivalry what is really harassment,

then feminists who engage in campaigns which appeal to the superior moral status of women are themselves endorsing the very
qualities which have been nurtured by patriarchal societies.

This point is not new. It is made by Alison Jaggar in *Feminist Politics and Human Nature* when she remarks that radical feminists

> glorify women precisely for the same reasons that men have
> scorned and sometimes feared them: in so doing they give special
> value to women's reproductive functions and to the psychologi-
> cal characteristics that have distinguished women and men. By
> grasping the nettle so firmly, radical feminists intend not only to
> crush the sting but even to produce some celebratory wine.[15]

The revaluing of qualities nurtured in situations of inequality or
oppression is common both to those who supported the moral purity
campaigns of the nineteenth century and to those who now endorse
the morality of care which underpins Dworkin and MacKinnon's
anti-pornography campaign. In the former case, the suppression
of sexuality was an explicit aim; and in the latter case it is a close
concomitant of the demand for relationships which are non-
hierarchical, since Dworkin and MacKinnon doubt whether hetero-
sexual sex ever is non-hierarchical. MacKinnon reports: 'The *Diary* of
the Barnard conference on sexuality pervasively equates sexuality
with "pleasure" . . . As if pleasure, and how to get it, rather than
dominance and how to end it, is the "overall" issue sexuality presents women.'[16] And other recent writings in feminist theory, notably
Carole Pateman's important book, *The Sexual Contract*, concur with
the belief that the root of women's oppression lies in men's sexual
power over them. Pateman writes: 'the origin of political right must
either be repressed or reinterpreted if the creation of civil society
is to be represented as a victory over patriarchy, and the sexual
contract is to remain hidden.'[17] On her account, the origin of political right lies in man's sexual conquest of woman, the 'primal act'
of rape, which both pre-dates and legitimizes political right and civil
society.

In all these cases, therefore, the call for a revaluation is not simply
a call for the recognition of different moral values; it is also, and
crucially, a demand for the suppression of male sexuality. For the
superior moral value of women is defined by reference to its mirror

image – the sexual appetitiveness of men. And the intolerance associated with social purity movements is therefore not contingent, but necessary. It follows straightforwardly from the understanding of heterosexuality as the means whereby men keep women in a state of subjugation.

As I have said, the demand for a revaluation of women's moral qualities is not new. Nor is it something from which I entirely dissent: the atomism of contemporary liberal theory has been well documented in recent years, and there is indeed something tiresome about its insistent emphasis on the importance of justice to the exclusion of all other virtues. If feminist moral and political theory has raised the profile of virtues other than justice, it has served philosophy well. What is troubling, however, is the precise form which the revaluation has taken. In its identification of existing problems, it acknowledges the extent to which people's qualities may be formed (for good or ill) by the society in which they find themselves. But it then accepts those qualities as the basis for a new and better society. Indeed, it accepts them as the destination of the utopian urge. On this account, the Promised Land is a gift outright. But it is given *to the oppressed*. No reference is made to any possible changes in people as they journey towards the promised land, nor is it envisaged that there will be any relationship of interdependence between the character of the people and the fulfilment of the promise. Release from oppression consists entirely in the suppression or alteration of male sexuality.

Thus, from a feminist perspective, the difficulty with communitarianism is not simply that it has no account to give of how we may attain critical distance from the society in which we find ourselves, it is also that, when coupled with a messianic aproach to politics, it delivers a society in which women retain those qualities which were originally generated by oppression. The paradox which ensues, and which Atwood exposes in *The Handmaid's Tale*, is that the resulting society is a utopia of the oppressed. Similarly, Dworkin and Mackinnon's analysis draws attention to the different moral voice in which women speak, but the superiority of that voice derives from the contrast drawn between it and a male voice, which is construed as essentially a voice of sexual domination and conquest. Improvement must therefore depend almost entirely upon the restriction of male sexuality, since any proposal for changes in women's morality or sexuality would undermine the status of the 'moral voice' originally appealed to.

These considerations have consequences for the kind of alternative utopian society envisaged by feminists. It has been remarked that although feminist theory has done much to identify the shortcomings of traditional political theory, it has been rather less successful in setting out its own practical proposals for political change. What I am suggesting is that this fact has a dual theoretical explanation: in identifying the problems inherent in modern political theory, feminists emphasize the close association between the sort of people we are and the sort of society we live in. They make much of the interdependence between people and their world, and this is their reason for rejecting atomistic liberalism. However, in describing a feminist future, those same feminists frequently ignore considerations of interdependence and revert to a static account of a feminist utopia – one which treats the future world as given and remains silent about the changes in women's character which might be consequent upon a change in their society. Yet more troubling, the assumption which underpins at least some feminist theory is that there is neither the need for, nor the possibility of, such change. Change is not needed because women's 'different' or 'moral' voice already expresses all that is best in human nature; and change is not possible because it would require an entirely different sexual order. Specifically, it would require the removal of hierarchical sexual relationships, and that can only be attained by the removal of men. Hence the assumption, common in feminist writing, that a genuine feminist utopia would be a female utopia. If, however, these are the consequences of traditional utopian and messianic thinking, how could the situation be improved by criticial or Exodus thinking? I turn now to this alternative.

Another country

I have suggested that a crucial distinction between Exodus and messianic thinking is that the former, but not the latter, implies a dynamic relationship between the world and the character of the people who inhabit that world. In the case of the original Exodus story this means that the nature of the Promised Land, when finally it is reached, is rather different from the land which was promised.

One important reason for this is that the moral and spiritual character of the promise (as distinct from its material character) depends crucially upon the people being a certain way. In material terms, the Promised Land will be a land 'flowing with milk and honey', but the material promise also has a moral and political dimension, for we are told that the people 'shall build houses and inhabit them; and they shall plant vineyards, and eat the fruit of them. They shall not build and another inhabit; they shall not plant and another eat.'[18] And again: 'they shall sit every man under his vine and under his fig tree; and none shall make them afraid.'[19]

In other words, the Promised Land is not simply a land of material plenty, but also a land which lacks exploitation and oppression. And again, there may be two facets to the removal of exploitation and oppression: one is the removal of exploitative and oppressive political institutions, the other is the transformation of the personality of the oppressed. The expression 'none shall make them afraid' implies *both* the removal of those social and political structures which engender fear, *and* the removal of fearfulness as a state of mind or quality of character. Morever, it implies that the one is conditional upon the other: improvement in the world is conditional upon improvement in the people. And so it turns out, for in the biblical Exodus the Israelites crossed Jordan only to find themselves, metaphorically at least, back in Egypt. By using their own freedom in order to oppress others, they did not inhabit a promised land, but a land of oppression – a land just like Egypt. And, as is the way of stories, this oppression was not simply one which they visited on others, but also one which they suffered themselves.

However, it is not only in stories that those who seek escape from oppression may yet find themselves oppressed. This, I take it, is part of the warning which Ronald Dworkin sounds against Catherine MacKinnon's proposals for the reform of pornography laws:

[Many feminists deplore MacKinnon's alliances] with right wing groups that have produced, for example, a Canadian censorship law that, as many had warned, has been used by conservative moralists to ban gay and lesbian literature by well-known authors, a book on racial injustice by the black feminist scholar, bell hooks, and, for a time, Andrea Dworkin's own feminist writing as well.

Perhaps MacKinnon should reflect on these suggestions that the censorship issue is not so simple-minded, so transparently gender-against-gender as she insists.[20]

The warning should not be read simply as a point about the difficulty of constructing pornography laws which cover only the 'right' material: *Hustler* but not *Ice and Fire*, *Stud* but not *Madame Bovary*. It is also a warning against messianic willingness to 'force the end', to attain a world without pornography by whatever means are necessary and with whatever allies are available. And that, in turn, is because the nature of the end will be partly determined by the character of the people who inhabit the end state. In order to clarify this point, I will make a few further remarks about the modern debate on pornography, and in the process, try to explain how Exodus thinking might alter the terms of that debate.

The first point to be made is that feminist thinking about pornography, when it adopts the Exodus pattern, will not be willing to 'force the end' in the sense of accepting assistance from any ally. This is because, for Exodus thinking, the end is not a predetermined state of affairs, a gift outright, but is dependent upon the character of people, which will change over time. Legal changes may of course be instrumental in the transformation, but they cannot be the end point, and to make them so is to assume in advance that one knows what moral perfection consists in. Like messianic thinking (of which I take MacKinnon's proposals to be an example), Exodus thinking aspires to a world in which there is no pornography, but unlike messianic thinking, it sees that state of affairs as essentially a relational one, dependent not only on the non-existence of certain kinds of publication, but also, and more importantly, on a change in their social meaning. A world without pornography will not be one in which certain kinds of depictions are no longer published, but rather one where their significance is radically transformed. This should not be an unfamiliar point to writers like MacKinnon, whose argument depends crucially upon the contention that pornographic material has a social meaning and is objectionable precisely because of the social meaning it carries in societies such as our own. She writes:

> Pornography sexualises rape, battery, sexual harassment prostitution and child sexual abuse; it thereby celebrates, promotes,

authorizes and legitimizes them . . . pornography's world of equality is a harmonious and perfectly balanced place. Men and women are perfectly complementary and perfectly bipolar. Women's desire to be fucked by men is equal to men's desire to fuck women.[21]

For her, pornography is not simply a set of representations arousing prurient interest; it is the main institutional channel through which the subordination of women is legitimized, indeed eroticized. And it rests upon the false belief that 'women's desire to be fucked by men is equal to men's desire to fuck women'. But why is this belief false? It is surely one thing to object to pornography's eroticization of rape, battery or sexual abuse, quite another to claim that *in general* sexual appetite divides neatly along gender lines. MacKinnon needs this second claim in order to make the moral case for anti-pornography legislation, but it is a considerable hostage to fortune, since it delivers her into the hands of the moral majority whose objection to pornography is not that it eroticizes sexual abuse, but that it eroticizes *sex*. In the end, this appears to be MacKinnon's objection too.

The claim that pornography has social meaning is central to feminist complaints against it. To this extent, MacKinnon is right to draw attention to what pornography says about women. And often what it does say is that they enjoy rape, abuse, violence and forced sex. But to deny this is not to deny that women have sexual desires just as strong as those of men. MacKinnon's assumption is that they do not, and that it is pornography which is responsible for creating the impression that they do. But why should we not make the opposite assumption: that women's sexual desires are just as strong as men's, and that it is pornography which is responsible for creating the impression that they are not? What would then be desired is, still and all, a world without pornography, but that would be attained not simply by restrictive legislation. It would require also that women find new ways of acknowledging their sexuality.

I am not here suggesting that the appropriate antidote to pornography is 'female pornography': in so far as pornography has a social meaning, that meaning cannot be changed simply by presenting mirror images of the existing meaning. Equally, however, the antidote cannot simply be changes in legislation, since these are not, on their own, sufficient to afford the transformation of character referred to above. On the contrary, and as proposed by MacKinnon, they imply that the character of women will remain essentially the same, only better protected. These two features of MacKinnon's proposals, a willingness to force the end and a denial of women's sexuality, display the essential elements of messianic thinking and lead inevitably to intolerance and oppression. Exodus thinking, by contrast, resists those conclusions because it is concerned to emphasize both the fact that a lengthy journey is necessary in order to arrive at the Promised Land, and the fact that, when we do arrive there, we will be significantly different people from the ones who originally set out. It will therefore see anti-pornography legislation as justified to the extent, and only to the extent, that it may be instrumental in increasing women's autonomy, and will not couple this with any assumption about the moral superiority of women's existing attitudes towards their own sexuality. This is not simply because such an assumption forges alliances between radical feminism and moral conservatism. It is also because existing attitudes are, by feminists' own lights, a product of exploitative and oppressive social arrangements. To give too much credence to them is to compound, not remove, the grounds for protecting rather than liberating women.

Because it recognizes that liberation requires more than the reversal of existing structures of hierarchy, this form of thinking will be less oppressive and intolerant than that proposed by MacKinnon. Because it insists upon the need for a change in character on the part of the oppressed, it will be less communitarian in its understanding of the relationship between people and their world. And because it acknowledges the way in which society shapes value, it will be better able than atomistic liberalism to identify the sources of oppression and also to resist replicating them. The land in which 'none shall be afraid' cannot be built on intolerant legal practices, but neither can it rest on the promise (or threat) that the great day will come when sexual desire disappears. Toleration for feminists, as for everyone else, must live in the twilight zone between the ruthless repression of all that we have been since the Fall, and the vain hope that there is another Eden which we may yet rediscover.

11
The Importance of Love in Rawls's Theory of Justice[1]

It is a familiar and much discussed question whether the disposition to act justly is one which can be commended to each and every individual as being in his or her self-interest. One of the most famous discussions of the question occurs in Hume's *A Treatise of Human Nature* and, while conceding that in an individual case a man may 'impoverish himself' by acting justly, Hume nevertheless concludes that:

> however single acts of justice may be contrary either to public or to private interest, 'tis certain that the whole plan or scheme is highly conducive and requisite both to the support of society and the well-being of every individual. 'Tis impossible to separate the good from the ill.[2]

For Hume, the damage which may be consequent upon single acts of justice is far outweighed by the social benefits accruing from the practice of justice, and since we cannot (collectively) enjoy the benefits without also (individually) rendering ourselves vulnerable to the perils, we have, on balance, reason to be just.

Hume's theme is echoed by John Rawls who, in an uncharacteristically lyrical passage of *A Theory of Justice*, acknowledges that the decision to preserve our sentiment of justice is one which may result in very great personal loss, or even ruin. Nevertheless, Rawls insists, the possibility of ruin is not simply that, for although the just man acknowledges the risks attached to preserving his sense of justice in hostile circumstances, and although 'it is true enough that for the sake of justice a man may lose his life where another would live to a later day, the just man does what, all things considered he most wants; in this sense he is not defeated by ill fortune, the possibility of which he foresaw'.[3]

Both Rawls and Hume acknowledge that acting justly may bring pain and suffering to the individual on specific occasions, but their characterizations of the individual who suffers through retaining a sense of justice are interestingly different. For Hume it is simply 'impossible to separate the good from the ill' and therefore, since the practice of justice has overwhelming social benefits, we must, as it were, take the rough with the smooth and recognize that there can be instances where justice turns out to be disadvantageous or damaging to us as individuals. On this understanding, we are simply gamblers, forced to concede that the favourite sometimes comes in last. Or martyrs, sacrificing ourselves on the altar of a greater social good.

For Rawls, however, we are neither gamblers nor martys for, having acknowledged that justice may on occasion bring suffering or even ruin in its wake, he goes on to insist that the just man is not thereby 'defeated'. Suffering and ruin are, it seems, distinct from defeat, and it is an implication of Rawls's characterization of the problem that the man who retains his sense of justice, and suffers as a consequence, far from being 'impoverished', is in fact, and in some way, vindicated. The precise way in which he is vindicated is expressed in the immediately following passage, where Rawls compares the hazards of justice to the hazards of love. He writes:

> those who love one another or acquire strong attachments to persons and to forms of life, at the same time become liable to ruin: their love makes them hostages to misfortune and the injustice of others . . . once we love we are vulnerable: there is no such thing as loving while being ready to consider whether to love, just like that. And the loves that hurt the least are not the best loves.[4]

This passage therefore promises a resolution, or at least a response, to an ancient philosophical problem: the problem of how we can commend justice to each and every individual while at the same time conceding that justice may, in some cases, result in suffering or ruin. Moreover, and most interestingly, it promises a resolution which depends neither on a conception of justice as merely the 'best bet' in a world which is always liable to upset our well-grounded expectations, nor as an institution whose beneficial consequences are purchased at the expense of the individuals who comply with it.

Rawls's argument rests upon an analogy between the hazards of justice and the hazards of love: we know that love may bring pain and humiliation, but we nevertheless commend it. To ask to be shown that each and every case of love is one which will bring happiness is to misunderstand the nature of love. Indeed, 'the loves that hurt the least are not the best loves'. And he suggests that we adopt a similar attitude towards justice, which can, he says, be understood as a special case of love: like love, justice is not invalidated by the acknowledgement that it may, on occasion, result in unhappiness or even in disaster.

Although Rawls never elaborates on this argument, and presents it only in the dying pages of *A Theory of Justice*, it seems to me to be one which is worth exploring further both because it promises a resolution to an ancient problem, and because that resolution may cast light on the problem of stability which is Rawls's focus in *Political Liberalism*. In the Introduction to *Political Liberalism* Rawls identifies the differences between that work and *A Theory of Justice* as arising from the fact that the account of stability offered in Part III of *A Theory of Justice* is 'unrealistic and must be recast'.[5] He insists that all differences between the two works spring from the inadequacy of his earlier account of stability. However, I shall argue here that there is no such inadequacy and that Part III of *A Theory of Justice* contains the resources to provide a satisfactory answer to the problem of stability. Therefore, in so far as *Political Liberalism* is an attempt to make good the defects in the account of stability offered in Part III of *A Theory of Justice*, it is superfluous. To say this, of course, is not to say that *Political Liberalism* contains nothing of interest or importance.

I shall begin, therefore, by saying a bit more about the problem of stability which prompts Rawls to draw an analogy between love and justice. I shall then go on to draw out the analogy in some detail, and finally I shall suggest some ways in which it might inform our understanding of the motivation to justice and of Rawls's theory (or theories) of justice more generally.

The problem of stability

In both *Political Liberalism* and *A Theory of Justice* Rawls emphasizes that justice as fairness has two stages: the first is to work out a free-standing political conception for the basic structure of society; the second is to show that justice as fairness is stable. The problem of stability is the problem of showing that:

> given certain assumptions specifying a reasonable human psy-chology and the normal conditions of human life, those who grow up under just basic institutions acquire a sense of justice and a reasoned allegiance to those institutions sufficient to render them stable. Expressed another way, citizens' sense of justice, given their traits of character and interests as formed by living under a just basic structure, is strong enough to resist the normal tendencies to injustice. Citizens act willingly so as to give one another justice over time. Stability is secured by sufficient motivation of the appropriate kind acquired under just institutions.[6]

And similarly in *A Theory of Justice*:

> Now a well-ordered society is also regulated by its public concep-tion of justice. This fact implies that its members have a strong and normally effective desire to act as the principles of justice require . . . one conception of justice is more stable than another if the sense of justice that it tends to generate is stronger and more likely to override disruptive inclinations and if the institutions it allows foster weaker impulses and temptations to act unjustly.[7]

So having established the two principles of justice, Rawls still con-siders it necessary, even in a well-ordered society, to show that people will be motivated to act in accordance with them. Additionally, he aims to show that, in a well-ordered society, the motivation to justice will win out over other, competing inclinations. The sense of justice motivates, and it motivates more strongly than anything else. How, then, does it motivate?

In answer to this question Rawls denies the plausibility of any appeal to the 'purely conscientious act', where that is understood as the claim that 'the highest moral motive is the desire to do what is right and just simply because it is right and just, no other description being appropriate',[8] and prefers instead an appeal to 'the Kantian interpretation' according to which 'men express their nature as free and equal rational beings' by acting justly.[9] The denial of conscientiousness emphasizes Rawls's belief that there must be some motivational story, additional to the bare assertion that the thing in question is right; the appeal to the Kantian interpretation emphasizes his belief that the motivational story must be one which shows justice to be congruent with the agent's own good. As Brian Barry glosses it: 'recoiling from the doctrine of the pure conscientious act, Rawls commits himself to the ancient doctrine that no act can be regarded as rational unless it is for the good of the agent to perform it.'[10]

It is not entirely clear whether Barry believes that these two are mutually exclusive and jointly exhaustive alternatives, but he implies that the Kantian 'infection' can best be stemmed by a more sophisticated understanding of conscientiousness, and devotes much energy to undermining Rawls's objections to the doctrine of the purely conscientious act. However, this is not the only alternative: we might reject both conscientiousness (understood as 'the desire to do what is right simply because it is right, no other description being appropriate') and congruence (understood as the belief that 'no act can be regarded as rational unless it is for the good of the agent to perform it'), simply by insisting that there is indeed an additional motivational story to be told, but that it need not be one which appeals to the agent's own good.

There are, therefore, not two possibilities, but three: conscientiousness (the desire to do what is right simply because it is right); non-congruence (the desire to do what is right for some reason distinct from the bare acknowledgement that it is right); and congruence (the desire to do what is right for reasons associated with the good of the agent). Why does Rawls reject the first two accounts in favour of the last? More specifically, does Rawls include the second within his definition of the purely conscientious act, or not? In order to answer these questions, we need to pay careful attention to what exactly Rawls understands the doctrine of the purely conscientious act to be.

Conscientiousness

Rawls's problem, to recall, is that of showing what will motivate people to act justly once they have identified and accepted the two principles, and his denial that the doctrine of conscientiousness can provide an adequate explanation is closely associated with his reading of Ross:

> Ross holds that the sense of right is a desire for a distinct (and unanalyzable) object, since a specific (and unanalyzable) property characterizes actions that are our duty. The other morally worthy desires, while indeed desires for things necessarily connected with what is right, are not desires for the right as such. But on this interpretation the sense of right lacks any apparent reason: it resembles a preference for tea rather than coffee.[11]

It should be said straight away that this is a highly idiosyncratic intepretation both of Ross in particular and of intuitionism generally. Normally, intuitionism is understood as a theory about how we recognize something as right or wrong, not as a theory about what motivates us to act on that recognition. Indeed, one of the central problems attendant upon Ross's intuitionism is precisely that it appears to provide no link between recognition and motivation. As Jonathan Dancy puts it:

> For Ross, our moral attitudes are beliefs, and so depend on the existence of a suitable desire if they are to motivate us to action. So if our moral opinions are to make any difference to how we act, there must be present in us also something like a general desire to do the good – a desire which we might comprehensibly have lacked. And if we had lacked it, we would still have been able to tell what is right and what is wrong; we would merely have found in the distinction between right and wrong nothing that made any difference to how we felt called on to behave. Morality, being purely factual, is thus deprived of any intrinsic relation to conduct in a way the critics found easy to ridicule.[12]

So on the standard interpretation, intuitionism does not identify the sense of right with any desire at all, and in this respect Rawls's reading of Ross is highly atypical. As a result, it is not clear whether Rawls objects to Ross's theory on the grounds that it (allegedly) construes the sense of right as itself a *desire*, or whether he objects to it on the grounds that it construes the sense of right as a desire *for a simple, unanalysable property*. That is to say, it is not clear whether the doctrine of the purely conscientious act is unacceptable to Rawls because it claims that the recognition of something as good (or right, or just) contains its own motivational trigger within it, or whether it is unacceptable because it holds that goodness (or rightness, or justice) is simple and unanalysable. If it is the latter, then Rawls's objection to conscientiousness is really an objection to a very specific account of moral motivation (i.e. Ross's account); if the former, then it is a more general objection to any claim that the recognition of something as right contains its own motivational trigger.[13]

Brian Barry appears not to distinguish between these possibilities. Against Rawls he argues that a suitably sophisticated interpretation of conscientiousness need not render moral action 'utterly capricious' and commends Scanlon's claim that 'the source of motivation which is directly triggered by the belief that an action is wrong is the desire to justify oneself to others on grounds which they could not reasonably reject'.[14] He then goes on to argue that the Scanlonian account serves both to provide reasons for acting morally and to be an example of the doctrine of the purely conscientious act: 'it is quite natural to say that the thought that something is the right thing to do is what motivates us to act rightly. I take this to be precisely the proposition that Rawls objects to.'[15] It is indeed the proposition which Rawls objects to, but what remains uncertain is whether Rawls objects to it because right is construed as simple and unanalysable (literally 'without reason'), or whether he objects to it because right (even when it accommodates reasons) is construed as a direct motivational trigger. By invoking the Scanlonian interpretation Barry can deflect the allegation that conscientiousness renders morality capricious, but this still will not satisfy Rawls, who is concerned to show not only that there are reasons for moral action, but also that those reasons are congruent with the agent's own good.

Congruence

If, then, the real dispute is about congruence rather than conscientiousness, what is to be said in favour of Rawls's claim that the sentiment of justice must be shown to be in keeping with the good of the agent who has it? In *A Theory of Justice* he writes, 'the problem is whether the regulative desire to adopt the standpoint of justice belongs to a person's own good when viewed in the light of the thin theory and with no restrictions on information',[16] and goes on to note that this is distinct from the problem of egoism: 'we are concerned with the goodness of the settled desire to take up the standpoint of justice. I assume that the members of a well-ordered society already have this desire. The question is whether this regulative sentiment is consistent with their good.'[17]

So we are not here concerned with the egoist or the amoralist who raises the question: 'Why should I be just?'. Rather the problem is to assure the person who already has a fixed and settled desire to act in accordance with justice that that desire is one which is congruent with his or her good.

Why should we think that such a thing can or must be shown? Barry, for one, denies that it can. Having demonstrated that the pure conscientious act need not be capricious, but can furnish reasons for action, he goes on to express his perplexity at the insistence that those reasons must also be congruent with the agent's own good. He writes:

> Suppose that I form the view that it would contribute to my good to take a trip around the world, and that I then find that this would cost more than my resources permit. (Let us follow Rawls in assuming that I live in a just society, so my budget limit corresponds to the one imposed by just economic institutions.) Instead of simply concluding that I cannot justly take the trip (while continuing to believe that taking it would be for my good), I am told by Rawls that I must somehow persuade myself that it would not be for my good at all . . . this is the absurdity into which Rawls is led by his rejection of the 'doctrine of the purely conscientious act'.[18]

And Scanlon, too, appears to concur with this diagnosis when he writes (albeit in a rather different context) that 'a theory of moral motivations need not show that the moral truth gives anyone who knows it a reason to act which appeals to that person's present desires or to the advancement of his or her interests'.[19]

The situation, then, seems to be this: in order to solve the problem of stability, we must show that people who live in a well-ordered society have reasons for cultivating and acting upon their sense of justice. Those reasons, however, must be ones which display justice as congruent with the agent's own good, for if they do not, then stability is jeopardized. Barry clearly believes that the search for congruence is deeply misguided, and he has two objections to it, both of which are implicit in the quotation given above. The first is that an insistence on congruence is deeply counterintuitive: it implies that, where the dictates of justice and self-interest conflict, it is not open to me simply to conclude that I cannot do the thing which would be for my own good. Rather, I must revise my understanding of what my good consists in. And this seems wrong. The second difficulty, and the one which appears to lead Rawls to renounce Part III of *A Theory of Justice*, is that the proof of congruence seems to require adherence to a strongly Kantian (and hence strongly metaphysical) understanding of the person: in order to show congruence, Rawls invokes the 'Kantian interpretation', according to which we are, by nature, free and equal rational beings. He is then able to claim that cultivating and endorsing the sense of justice as a regulative desire is a way (in fact *the* way) of expressing that nature and thus of realising our good. However, the argument has appeal only for those who concur in thinking of themselves as essentially free and equal rational beings. But to think of oneself in this way is to favour a comprehensive, and highly controversial, conception of the good. By invoking that conception in Part III of *A Theory of Justice* Rawls now believes that he has converted justice as fairness into a comprehensive doctrine or, at the very least, rendered the stability of justice as fairness dependent upon the acceptance of a comprehensive doctrine. What is needed, therefore, is a response to the problem of stability which is more than simply an appeal to the purely conscientious act (however interpreted), but less than the full blown Kantian interpretation.

To recap, then, the problem identified by Rawls may be unpacked in something like the following manner: in order to guarantee stability in a well-ordered society, we need to show that people have reasons for cultivating the disposition to justice. Moreover, we need to show that those reasons are more powerful than any reasons they might have for eschewing justice and acting on other dispositions.

So the disposition to justice cannot be explained adequately by invoking the alleged motivating power of justice as a simple, unanalysable property, nor can it be explained adequately by introducing a more sophisticated, Scanlonian, account of motivation, since this, too, fails to guarantee that the motivation to justice will be sufficiently strong to outweigh other, conflicting motivations. Therefore, in order to satisfy the stability requirement, what must be shown is that the agent has a very powerful motivation to act on his sense of justice – and presumably the most powerful motivation there can be is one which shows acting justly to be congruent with the agent's own good. Of course, Barry denies that this can be shown, and Rawls himself now thinks that it can only be shown by invoking a comprehensive account. However, in the next section I shall examine the analogy between love and justice in an attempt to offer a route to congruence which avoids comprehensiveness. It may be objected that this discussion assumes what is in fact still at issue, namely, that there is indeed a problem of congruence. However, one of the consequences of the argument of the next section is that, if successful, it will show that the problem of congruence is construed as such by Barry and others only because and insofar as they inerpret it in an unsatisfactory way.

Love and justice

In drawing the analogy between love and justice Rawls implies two things: first, that the disposition to justice, once adopted, cannot be given up simply because justice may result in pain or unhappiness: 'there is no such thing as loving while being ready to consider whether to love, just like that.'[20] Similarly, we must suppose, there is no such thing as having a disposition to act justly while being prepared to consider whether to be just on each and every occasion. To behave in that way is simply to fail to display the virtue of justice. In part, this is just a further articulation of Rawls's starting point: we are supposing that in a well-ordered society people do in fact have a disposition to act justly. We are not therefore attempting to answer the egoist's question: 'Why should I cultivate the disposition to justice?' Rather, our question is whether, once someone has the desire to be just, and has it as a regulative desire, it can be seen to be one which accords with his or her own good.

It is here that Rawls introduces the second consideration – the claim that 'the loves that hurt the least are not the best loves'. This suggests that what may be best (and best for the agent) is distinguishable from what brings the greatest balance of happiness over pain. But the difficulty with this is that it is a claim which needs to steer a precarious path between a familiar and uninteresting objection to egoistic hedonism and a controversial appeal to the doctrine of the 'true self', according to which there may be things which are in my real interest independent of whether I actually desire them, and even if I positively reject or avoid them. I take it that by making specific reference to love Rawls means to draw our attention to distinctive features of it: features which, once understood, can also inform our understanding of justice and help to create a space between egoistic hedonism and appeal to the true self. What are these features?

The first point to be made is that the analogy between love and justice casts doubt on the claim that Rawls need be adopting a straightforwardly Kantian position. As was noted earlier, Barry implies that the denial of conscientiousness brings with it a commitment to the Kantian doctrine of the true self, and Rawls himself refers to his own favoured solution to the problem of congruence as 'Kantian'. The matter cannot, however, be left at that. Kant, notoriously, was deeply suspicious of love, and in his moral theory the demands of right are opposed to the demands of love; they are certainly not to be compared with it. However, the reasons for Kant's 'misamorism' are instructive. He perceives love as essentially at odds with respect precisely because love exposes us to the ill-will of others and increases the chances of our being harmed by them. Thus he writes: 'the principle of mutual love admonishes men to come closer to one another; that of the respect they owe to one another, to keep themselves at a distance',[21] and he goes on to elaborate on this by claiming that the duty of love involves making another's ends my own (in so far as that is possible), whereas the duty of respect merely enjoins me not to use others as a means to my own ends. What is problematic (and dangerous) about love is that, in making another's ends my own, I render myself vulnerable. Should my friend turn out to be false, or should enmity develop between us, I will risk humiliation because I have given too much of myself to the other person. I have allowed him or her too much access to myself, and that knowledge may now be used as a weapon against me. Kant's advice, in short, is that we should treat our friends as though they may, at any moment, become our enemies.

Connectedly, he believes that even the requirements of a 'good' friendship are in tension with considerations of respect, and he explains this by citing the case in which one friend performs a favour for another. Of this he says:

> If one [friend] accepts a favour from the other, then he may well be able to count on equality in love, but not in respect; for he sees himself as obviously a step lower in so far as he is under an obligation without being able reciprocally to impose obligation . . . friendship is something so delicate that it is never for a moment safe from interruptions if it is allowed to rest on feelings and if this mutual sympathy and self-surrender are not subjected to principles or rules preventing excessive familiarity limiting mutual love by the requirements of respect.[22]

So friendship is often false and duplicitous, and even where it is not, it has the potential to become so. Moreover, even within a 'good' friendship there are reasons for retaining distance: by accepting friendship from another I risk damage from his ill-will should our friendship falter, and by offering friendship to another I make him beholden to me in a way which undermines equality of respect.

Clearly, all this sits ill with Rawls's claims that 'there is no such thing as loving while being ready to consider whether to love, just like that' and that 'the loves that hurt the least are not the best loves'. In fact, Kant's attitude to love and friendship seems to be precisely that they are to be considered as gambles and in this, as in all gambles, the prudent man will 'cover his bets'. We must always 'so conduct ourselves towards a friend that there is no harm done if he should turn into an enemy',[23] and what this means is that we should not allow friendship to extend so far, or so deep, as to expose us to pain and humiliation.

More generally, Kant's injunction seems to be that, in choosing and maintaining friendship, or in nurturing love for another, we must always remember that our own ends are distinct from, and potentially in conflict with, those of our friend. This is the reason why friendship and love are dangerous: they enable the friend who knows our ends to subvert them, thwart them or hold them up to ridicule. It is therefore the separateness of persons, and the distinctness of their different ends, which makes love perilous and 'risky' in Kant's eyes.

By contrast with Kant, Charles Fried proposes an understanding of love according to which:

> an important and perhaps the central conception of love between persons involves a notion of reciprocity . . . this must be formalized not in terms of a free renunciation of entitlements to pursue one's own interests in order to take up the beloved's interests as one's own, but rather in terms of a mutual sharing of interests . . . the two lovers surely make no claims on each other, yet what they do or give must be given in mutual recognition of the firm base of each other's personality. This interest which the lovers pursue having abandoned self-interest, is not simply the reciprocal pursuit of the other's self-interest in place of one's own. That would be an absurdity. There is rather a creation of love, a middle term, which is a new pattern or system of interests which both share and both value, in part at least just because it is shared . . . In this way reciprocal love represents a kind of resolution of the paradoxes of self-interest and altruism.[24]

Where Kant emphasizes the separateness of individuals, and the distinctness and difference which characterize their ends, Fried argues that one important feature of love is that it heralds the genesis of a distinct set, or system, of interests – ones which involve the abandonment of separate ends, yet which do not demand the mere submission of one person's interests to those of another. In loving another person, I cease to think exclusively in terms of my own interests and their consonance or conflict with the interests of the person I love. Rather, I acknowledge an additional set of interests which are 'ours' and which may, in turn, inform my understanding of what constitutes my own interest. Kant's warning that love renders us vulnerable to the ill-will of others ignores the possibility that there could be this creation of additional, shared interests, and he is therefore forced to conclude that when love goes badly, the individuals involved are simply hurt and damaged *as individuals*. They gambled that their lives would go better if they pursued a particular relationship, and the gamble failed.

If, however, we take seriously the analysis offered by Fried, there is a further possibility, which is that when love goes badly, we lose something beyond the mere realization of our own interests. He argues that people who love one another value things which are shared, and value them in part because they are shared. What is then lost when love fails is precisely that sense of what is 'ours'. Of course, such a loss is damaging to the interests of the individuals who suffer it, but it is not simply that. It is also the loss of something which transcended individual interest. By insisting that the loves that hurt the least are not the best loves, Rawls implies that we may avoid the perils of love only by avoiding the commitment which facilitates the creation of these shared interests. Ironically, he implies precisely what one of his critics has accused him of denying – that in such cases we know a good in common which we cannot know alone.[25]

A more general contrast can now be drawn between Kant and Rawls: whereas Rawls begins with a problem about justice (how it can be commended to each individual) and invokes the case of love to exemplify the point that we do not always think that pain and suffering unjustify or ruin us, Kant begins with a problem about love (how the vulnerability it implies can be minimized) and invokes the language of right to exemplify the possibility of loving while retaining respect. The differences between their two accounts reflect a different understanding of the separateness of persons and of the ends they pursue. Having once insisted on the distinctness of ends, Kant has no real escape from an understanding of love as something which is potentially disastrous to the agent who practises it. Conversely, it is by questioning that separateness that we may be able to present an alternative understanding of love and, by extension, an understanding of justice which promises a resolution to the paradoxes of self-interest and altruism. If we were to come to see justice as, like love, something which involves the transformation of existing interests and the creation of new, shared, interests, then we would be less inclined to judge every case of suffering through justice as a case of unmitigated disaster, and less inclined to think that every such case must unjustify the agent's commitment to acting justly. The problem now, however, is to provide a persuasive argument explaining why we should take love as primary in this way. Why ought we to construe justice as a special case of love, rather than (in Kantian fashion) seeing love as a threat to justice? Responding to this question will take us back to the problem of congruence and the different status accorded to it by Rawls on the one hand, and Barry and Scanlon on the other.

The priority of love and the problem of congruence

As we have seen, both Barry and Scanlon doubt that there is a problem of congruence. In 'Contractualism and Utilitarianism' Scanlon asks what we can expect a theory of morality to say about moral motivation, and he replies that such a theory 'need not show that the moral truth gives anyone who knows it a reason to act which appeals to that person's present desires or to the advancement of his or her interests'.[26] He provides an account of moral motivation in terms of our desire to justify ourselves to others, and Barry following him concludes that the insistence on congruence is simply 'an absurdity into which Rawls is led by his rejection of the "doctrine of the purely conscientious act"'.[27]

However, the claim that it is absurd to demand congruence between morality and self-interest is most plausible if we consider a short time-slice and a fairly brute interpretation of 'desire'. It is indeed unlikely that, at every given moment, the dictates of morality will coincide with the agent's immediate preferences, and even if we interpret the congruence requirement as one which relates to (longer-term) interests rather than to (current) desires, it seems altogether probable that an agent's interests and the requirements of morality will, from time to time, conflict.

However, these doubts about congruence have most persuasive force on the assumption that interests are clear and determinate: to ask which of two alternatives will better serve my interests is to suppose that I already have an idea (whether true or false) of what my interests are, and therefore a standard against which to measure and decide which course of action will be most efficacious in promoting them. It is to assume a model of life as like a path which forks, and where the question to be asked is: 'which of these two paths will lead to greater happiness or fulfilment?' Once the question is put in that form, we have no guarantee that the answer to it will coincide with answers to questions about acting justly or morally well. And indeed it is in precisely that form that both Barry and Hume before him address the question of congruence.

The model is, however, too simple: our lives are not like paths which fork, and the assumption that they are may be one which misrepresents the problem of congruence and at the same time implies an impoverished picture of what it is to perceive something as consonant with one's good. The following example may help to explain this point: as a young person I may fervently desire academic success and fame, and I may also know that marriage to this person, whom I love, will bring with it an alteration in my conception of my interests such that, in middle age, I shall be content with domesticity and scorn the ambition which now I nurture. I may see my future self as dull and complacent, while simultaneously acknowledging that my future self will look back with fond affection on what it will then perceive as the misplaced and shallow ambition of youth. From which perspective, then, am I to decide whether it would best serve my interests to marry? To judge exclusively from my present motivations is not only to privilege the present over possible futures in a way which stands in need of justification, it is also to ignore the oddity of viewing decisions within a life as parts of a 'game plan'. In playing a game such as chess, I aim to win, and the question of which move I should make next is determined by that aim. In life, however, there need be no such single aim determining which move, or which decision, is the best one. Indeed, it is only rather unusual lives which are correctly characterized as lives led in the pursuit of a specific and constant aim. For most of us, aims change consequent upon earlier decisions, and what I deem to be valuable, or to be in my interest is, in part, a function of choices I have made and decisions I have taken along the way. Thus, in the example given above, my youthful decision to marry is not (we must hope) simply a strategic decision taken in the belief that it will advance my interests. Indeed, to have that reason for marrying would bespeak a bizarre, even corrupt, understanding of the nature of love and the significance of marriage. Rather, the decision is one which itself has implications for what my interests will be. This, then, is not a decision taken in strategic pursuit of an antecedently existing aim; it is a decision which is itself formative and transformative of my aims.[28]

But if this is right, then it has consequences for the denial that there is a problem of congruence. Barry thinks there is no reason to suppose that acting morally must coincide with a person's present desires or the advancement of his or her interests, and one reason for resisting any appeal to congruence is that it appears to open the door to a doctrine of the true self, for if morality does not coincide with the agent's actual desires or perceived interests, then it seems that congruence can be attained only by postulating some objective good, independent of, and possibly in conflict with, the agent's actual desires. But to countenance this possibility is to admit the 'Kantian infection'. However, what the analogy with love suggests is that the specification of an agent's good, when viewed in the context of his or her life as a whole, may be more malleable than is supposed by Barry, and if this is true, then the dangers of congruence may be less threatening.

The malleability of an agent's good is implicit in the recognition that some decisions themselves serve to alter our understanding of what constitutes our good, and it follows from this that appeal to the agent's good need not be a simple choice between existing desires and objective interest. The fact that love can alter our aims implies that there need be no single, predetermined specification of what constitutes the agent's good and, *a fortiori*, no single predetermined way of attaining it. On the other hand, however, the example also implies that our good is not to be identified simply with existing desire since, in making decisions within my life, I take account not only of what I do now desire, but also of the value of those desires. The case of love therefore provides us with an example of the symbiosis between existing desire and 'objective' value, which does not imply that the agent's good is determined, nor that it is determined wholly externally. It therefore provides a sense in which appeal to congruence need not admit the 'Kantian infection'.

The analogy with love also serves a further purpose in providing a response to those who see the demand for congruence as misplaced. As I have noted already, Scanlon argues that the moral motivation is properly characterized as a desire to justify oneself to others on grounds which they could not reasonably reject. However, in addition to justifying oneself to others one might also want to justify to oneself. Indeed Scanlon himself hints at this, albeit fleetingly, in his recognition that the agent will be dissatisfied if others are convinced

by a justification which he himself knows to be spurious, or (connectedly) if others are not persuaded by a justification which the
agent knows to be adequate.[29] This suggests that there is a sense in
which justifying to oneself has moral primacy since, in the end, the
ability to justify to others is to be tested by reference to the ability
to justify to oneself. In the final analysis, Scanlon is indifferent as to
whether other people do *as a matter of fact* accept one's justification;
his concern is with whether the agent himself believes that the action
is justifiable, and this implies either that justifying to oneself has
primacy, or that the concept of reasonableness must bear a great deal
of philosophical weight. Either way, though, the desire to justify
oneself to others is not the foundational concept. To put the point
provocatively (and perhaps slightly unfairly), the objection to Rawls's
congruence requirement is that in order to avoid egoistic hedonism
it must invoke a Kantian doctrine of the true self. But it can equally
be objected to a Scanlonian account of moral motivation that
in order to avoid condoning spurious justifications which are *as a
matter of fact* accepted by others, it too must appeal to a very robust,
even Kantian, conception of the reasonable. Scanlon's invocation of
the reasonable, if it is not simply an appeal to what people do in
fact find reasonable, is every bit as contentious as Rawls's appeal to
the agent's good. There is, however, a more constructive point to be
made here, which again involves considering the defining characteristics of love and setting them in the context of an account of
justification.

In 'The Importance of What We Care About' Harry Frankfurt notes
that reason and love are similar in that both entail selflessness: the
person who is bound by the requirements either of love or of reason
is, as it were, 'seized' by the object, 'the object captivates him. He is
guided by its characteristics rather than primarily by his own'.
However, love and reason also differ in that the claims of reason,
unlike the claims of love, are impersonal:

> they are not limited to the person who makes them; rather, it is
> implicit that anyone who disagrees with the claims must be mis-
> taken. A declaration of love is a personal matter, on the other
> hand, because the person who makes it does not thereby commit
> himself to supposing that anyone who fails to love what he does
> has somehow gone wrong.[30]

Frankfurt goes on to draw a general conclusion from this, which is that betraying the thing we love is distinct from failing in a moral duty. If I fail in a moral duty, then consistency requires that I condemn morally anyone else who acts similarly. However, where I betray the thing I love, I am not required to universalize in the same way and, most importantly, I do not conceive of my failure as involving an inability to justify to others. Rather, I conceive of it as betraying myself. This suggestion therefore draws our attention to a limitation on the scope of Scanlon's justificatory enterprise, even if we assume it to be capable of overcoming the difficulties mentioned earlier. Frankfurt writes:

> If a mother who is tempted to abandon her child finds that she simply cannot do that, it is probably not because she knows (or even because she cares about) her duty. It is more likely because of how she cares about the child, and about herself as its mother, than because of any recognition on her part that abandoning the child would be morally wrong ... Especially with respect to those we love and with respect to our ideals, we are liable to be bound by necessities which have less to do with our adherence to the principles of morality than with integrity or consistency of a more personal kind ... In a sense which a strictly ethical analysis cannot make clear, what they [the necessities] keep us from violating are not our duties or our obligations, but ourselves.[31]

Of course, to abandon one's child would be to fail in a moral duty, but the point here is that the mother herself is unlikely to perceive her action in that way, and equally unlikely to desist on those grounds. Indeed, we might even be tempted to say that a mother who did desist because it was her duty would have a defective understanding of what is involved in being a mother (just as the person who married in order to further their own life plan would have a defective understanding of what is involved in being a husband or wife). But whatever the truth of this, Frankfurt's central point is that there is a distinction between acting from moral obligation and acting from an ideal of personal integrity, and the difference lies partly in the centrality of the idea of betraying oneself.

To be guided by an ideal is to conceive of oneself in a certain way, and it is for that reason that violating the ideal is felt as a betrayal of oneself. Its being felt in that way is, moreover, prior to and independent of any thought about one's ability or otherwise to justify oneself to others. From the mother's point of view, her inability to justify to others her decision to abandon her child is largely irrelevant to her assessment of her own action. It is, I suggest, this thought which is implicit in Rawls's description of the desire to act justly as 'a desire to conduct oneself in a certain way above all else, a striving that contains within itself its own priority . . . for this sentiment [the sentiment of justice] reveals what the person is, and to compromise it is not to achieve for the self free reign but to give way to the contingencies and accidents of the world'.[32]

What is implicit in both Frankfurt and Rawls, therefore, is an assertion of the priority of being a certain sort of person. Frankfurt identifies the distinction between moral obligation and personal ideal as a distinction between justifying to others and justifying to oneself but, as his own example indicates, there can be cases in which what is (uncontroversially) a moral obligation is conceived by the agent as an ideal of personal integrity. By drawing the analogy with love, Rawls appears to be urging just this conversion of moral duty into personal ideal in the case of justice. He appears to be suggesting that, when held as a fully regulative sentiment, justice is something which moulds and shapes our other desires, just as love moulds and shapes our desires. Like love, justice can have a transformative quality. Like love, it can be understood as a reflection of the agent's desire to be a certain way, and its denial or betrayal will be best characterized not as a failure to justify to others, but as a betrayal of oneself and what one stands for.

Love, justice and stability

How do these considerations assist in responding to the question with which I began: the question of whether the disposition to act justly is one which can be commended to each and every individual as being in his or her own interest? How, in particular, do they assist in responding to that question without invoking a doctrine of the true self, or converting justice as fairness into a comprehensive doctrine and thus, as Rawls believes, failing to provide an adequate answer to the problem of stability?

My suggestion has been that the analogy between love and justice, when fully spelled out, can serve to cast doubt upon the simple denial of congruence favoured by Scanlon and Barry. This denial appears most plausible on the assumption that our lives are like paths which fork, and our decisions are decisions about which fork will better promote our happiness or satisfy our interests. However, this model obscures an important sense in which decisions in a life are not always merely strategic, nor are they taken in pursuit of an end which is pre-determined. They are, rather, constitutive and transformative of our ends. Nevertheless, the ways in which love serves to alter our ends does not presuppose that there is some entirely external and 'objective' criterion of the agent's good, for in making decisions of this transformative sort, the agent is (part) creator of her own life and of the ends which will characterize it. This possibility – the possibility that ends are malleable but not entirely externally determined, is part of what is implicit in the analogy between justice and love.

The second strand of the argument, however, draws attention to a different aspect of the analogy between love and justice. It suggests that justifying one's actions to others is ultimately parasitic on justifying one's actions to oneself. Indeed, Scanlon's account itself contains an implicit acknowledgement of this and I have suggested that without that acknowledgement, his theory must ultimately appeal to a highly contentious conception of the reasonable. More generally, the distinction between justifying to others and justifying to oneself signals a contrast between moral obligation and personal ideal, where the latter represents some feature of the agent which she believes to be constitutive of what she is. This distinction enables us to see how and why the rejection of the model of life as like a path which forks need not entail that 'anything goes', for the agent will still be guided by some ideals, some conception of the sort of person she is and the kinds of values she cannot neglect without betraying herself.

However, it may be objected that this conversion of justice into a personal ideal undermines the justificatory dimension of Rawls's account. It creates a space between congruence and the doctrine of the true self only by transforming justice into something which motivates at the individual level, but which cannot provide interpersonal justification. If what matters in the explanation of motivation is 'being true to myself', then justifying to others disappears. And this is odd in a theory of justice whose main purpose was to provide a form of justification which could be offered to others without invoking personal commitments or ideals.

Two responses may be made to this objection: the first is simply a reminder of the reason for introducing the analogy between love and justice in the first place. In both *A Theory of Justice* and *Political Liberalism* Rawls emphasizes that justice as fairness has two stages: the first is to work out a free-standing conception for the basic structure of society; the second is to show that justice as fairness is stable. The former we might dub the 'justificatory' stage; while the latter (at least in *A Theory of Justice*) is the 'motivational' stage. It is in connection with the motivational stage of the enterprise that the analogy between love and justice is drawn, and Rawls takes the justificatory project to have been completed in the earlier part of the book. So interpersonal justification is not threatened by the analogy between love and justice, since it is no part of the purpose of that analogy to provide justification. Rather, the aim is to show why, having been persuaded by the justification, the agent would be motivated to act. Thus, in the example taken from Fried, we have a case where the mother's motivation is explained by reference to her sense of what it is to be a mother (her commitment to the ideal of being a good mother), whereas the justification of her action will be given by reference to her moral obligations.

The second response concerns the precise way in which we are to understand the status given to love in Rawls's theory. Rawls, in fact, says very little about this, but I have suggested that we might plausibly interpret love as an ideal. In saying this, I do not mean to imply that it is a mere personal sentiment or preference, much less that it is capricious or unreliable. On the contrary, drawing out the analogy between love and justice illuminates the sense in which both are (or may be) guiding principles in the lives of individuals, principles which inform their actions and, as Rawls himself puts it, 'reveal what the person is'.[33]

However, both these responses depend upon a distinction between the justificatory and the motivational. The analogy between love and justice has been discussed as part of Rawls's attempt to fill the gap between accepting the principles of justice and being motivated to act on them, and in the final section of *A Theory of Justice* his main aim is to demonstrate that those who have accepted the principles will be motivated to act on them because they will find them to be congruent with their own good. In *Political Liberalism*, however, the argument takes a different turn, and Rawls now focuses on the variety of reasonable but competing comprehensive conceptions of the good which characterize modern society. His question is not 'why should people who accept the two principles be motivated to act on them?', rather it is, 'how can we justify the two principles to people who have comprehensive conceptions of the good which conflict with them?' And he goes on to assert that 'justice as fairness is not reasonable in the first place unless in a suitable way it can win its support by addressing each citizen's reason, as explained within its own frame-work'.[34] So now the problem of stability becomes part of the justificatory project, not part of the motivational project, and Rawls seems to see himself as driven back to the question of justification in part, at least, because he believes that the motivational story told in Part III of *A Theory of Justice* was one which relied upon a comprehensive conception of the good.

Some commentators have concurred with this diagnosis, and have seen the Kantian interpretation and the appeal to congruence as the point at which *A Theory of Justice* goes badly wrong. They therefore urge Rawls to jettison the Kantian interpretation, abandon the aspiration to congruence, and thus render the original theory immune to allegations of comprehensiveness.[35] It has been my aim in this chapter to suggest that that is over-hasty. The sense of justice can be shown to be for the good of the agent who endorses it without degenerating into absurdity and without invoking an objectionably Kantian doctrine of the true self. Via the analogy between love and justice Rawls makes an important and persuasive contribution to moral psychology and the theory of moral motivation. That he cannot also use that story to provide an account of political legitimacy is unsurprising and not, in my view, a reason for lamentation, much less a reason for declaring the final part of *A Theory of Justice* to be unsatisfactory or absurd.

Notes

Introduction

1. Judith Shklar, *Ordinary Vices*, Cambridge, Mass., The Belknap Press, 1984, p. 233.

Chapter 1 When the Kissing Had to Stop: Passion in the Thought of Mary Wollstonecraft

1. Miriam Brody, 'Mary Wollstonecraft: Sexuality and Women's Rights', in Dale Spender (ed.) *Feminist Theorists*, London, The Women's Press, 1983, p. 41.
2. Mary Wollstonecraft, *A Vindication of the Rights of Woman*, ed. Sylvana Tomaselli, Cambridge, Cambridge University Press, p. 100.
3. Wollstonecraft, *A Vindication of the Rights of Woman*, p. 259.
4. As quoted in William Godwin, *Memoirs of the Author of 'The Rights of Woman'*, ed. Richard Holmes, Harmondsworth, Penguin, 1987, p. 45.
5. Claire Tomalin, *The Life and Death of Mary Wollstonecraft*, London, Weidenfeld and Nicolson, 1974, p. 235.
6. Tomalin, *The Life and Death of Mary Wollsonecraft*, p. 238.
7. Wollstonecraft, *A Vindication of the Rights of Woman*, p. 127.
8. Sylvanan Tomaselli, Introduction to *A Vindication of the Rights of Woman*, p. xxv.
9. Jean-Jacques Rousseau, *Emile*, London, Dent, Everyman Library, 1974.
10. Rousseau, *Emile*, pp. 321ff.
11. *A Vindication of the Rights of Woman*, p. 98.
12. *The Works of Mary Wollstonecraft*, New York, New York University Press, 1989, Vol. 6, 'Letters to Imlay', Letter II, p. 369.
13. Wollstonecraft, *A Vindication of the Rights of Woman*, p. 99.
14. *The Works of Mary Wollstonecraft*, Letter LVI, p. 420.
15. Valerie Bryson, *Feminist Political Theory*, London, Macmillan, 1992, pp. 25–6.
16. Tomalin, *The Life and Death of Mary Wollstonecraft*, Chapter 12; Eleanor Flexner, *Mary Wollstonecraft*, Harmondsworth, Penguin, 1972, p. 192.
17. *The Works of Mary Wollstonecraft*, Letter II, p. 370.
18. *The Works of Mary Wollstonecraft*, Letter XLII, p. 407.
19. *The Works of Mary Wollstonecraft*, Letter LXVII, p. 428.
20. Carole Pateman, 'The Disorder of Women', in Pateman, *The Disorder of Women*, Oxford and Cambridge, Polity, 1989, p. 18.
21. *The Works of Mary Wollstonecraft*, Letter LXXV, p. 434.
22. This essay was first published in *The Historian*, June 1994.

Chapter 2 John Stuart Mill and Harriet Taylor on Women and Marriage

1. References to *The Subjection of Women* and *The Enfranchisement of Women* are to the Virago edition, London, 1983. References in square brackets are to the Collected Works edition of *The Subjection of Women, Essays on Equality, Law, and Education*, Vol. XXI, Toronto, 1984.
2. Michael St J. Packe, *The Life of John Stuart Mill*, London, Secker and Warburg, 1954, p. 492.
3. Ann Robson, 'No Laughing Matter: John Stuart Mill's Establishment of Women's Suffrage as a Parliamentary Question', *Utilitas*, 2, 1, 1990, p. 101.
4. Packe, *The Life of John Stuart Mill*, p. 495.
5. James Fitzjames Stephen, *Liberty, Equality, Fraternity*, ed. R.J. White, Cambridge, Cambridge University Press, 1967, pp. 190–1.
6. All quotations as cited in Packe, *The Life of John Stuart Mill*, pp. 495ff.
7. Fitzjames Stephen, *Liberty, Equality, Fraternity*, pp. 196–7.
8. Kate Soper, Introduction to the Virago edition of *The Subjection of Women and the Enfranchisement of Women*, p. viii.
9. Julia Annas, 'Mill and the Subjection of Women', *Philosophy*, 52, 1977, p. 191.
10. Carole Pateman, *The Sexual Contract*, Oxford and Cambridge, Polity, 1988, pp. 160–3.
11. *The Subjection of Women*, pp. 1–2 [p. 261].
12. p. 177 [p. 336].
13. Stefan Collini, Introduction to *John Stuart Mill, Collected Works, Vol. XXI: Essays on Equality, Law and Education*, Toronto, Toronto University Press, 1984, p. xv.
14. As quoted in Alice S. Rossi (ed.), *John Stuart Mill and Harriet Taylor: Essays on Sex Equality*, Chicago, Chicago University Press, 1970, p. 35.
15. Phyllis Rose, *Parallel Lives: Five Victorian Marriages*, Harmondsworth, Penguin, 1985, p. 15.
16. Gertrude Himmelfarb, *Of Liberty and Liberalism: The Case of John Stuart Mill*, New York, Knopf, 1974.
17. Pateman *The Sexual Contract*, p. 160.
18. As quoted in Soper, Introduction, p. xiv, n. 14.
19. *The Enfranchisement of Women*, pp. 26–30; p. 37.
20. Rossi, *John Stuart Mill and Harriet Taylor*, p. 85.
21. Rossi, *John Stuart Mill and Harriet Taylor*, p. 70.
22. Rossi, *John Stuart Mill and Harriet Taylor*, p. 70.
23. Alison Jaggar, *Feminist Politics and Human Nature*, Brighton, Harvester, 1983, p. 264.
24. 'Early Essay on Marriage and Divorce' in Rossi, *John Stuart Mill and Harriet Taylor*, p. 85.
25. *The Subjection of Women*, p. 27 [p. 271].
26. *The Subjection of Women*, p. 150 [p. 324].

27. *The Enfranchisement of Women*, pp. 38, 24.
28. Jaggar, *Feminist Politics*, p. 97.
29. Jaggar, *Feminist Politics*, p. 95ff.
30. F.R. Leavis (ed.), *Mill on Bentham and Coleridge*, Cambridge, Cambridge University Press, 1980, p. 9.
31. J.S. Mill, *Autobiography*, ed., J. Stillinger, Oxford, Oxford University Press, 1985, p. 89.
32. *Autobiography*, p. 106.
33. Annas, 'Mill and the Subjection of Women', p. 184.
34. Shulamith Firestone, *The Dialectic of Sex*, London, The Women's Press, 1979.
35. William Wordsworth, *The Prelude*, ed. Ernest de Selincourt, Oxford, Oxford University Press, 1959, XIII, 169–72.
36. This essay was first published in *Utilitas*, Vol. 6, No. 2, 1994, pp. 287–299.

Chapter 3 The Practical and the Pathological

1. L.W. Beck, *A Commentary on Kant's Critique of Practical Reason*, Chicago, University of Chicago Press, 1960, Chapter XI.
2. Jonathan Bennett, *Kant's Dialectic*, Cambridge, Cambridge University Press, 1974, p. 195.
3. Bernard Williams, 'Morality and the Emotions', as reprinted in Williams, *Problems of the Self*, Cambridge, Cambridge University Press, 1973, p. 228.
4. Williams, 'Morality and the Emotions'.
5. Kant, *The Critique of Pure Reason*, A534/B562.
6. Kant, *Critique of Practical Reason*, 100.
7. Peter Winch, 'Moral Integrity', *Inaugural Lecture*, King's College, London, pp. 12–13.
8. P.H. Nowell-Smith, *Ethics*, Harmondsworth, Penguin, 1954, p. 247.
9. Kant, *Groundwork*, 398.
10. F.M. Mayor, *The Rector's Daughter*, Harmondsworth, Penguin, 1973, p. 18.
11. Kant, *Groundwork*, 399.
12. Kant, *Lectures on Ethics*, London, Methuen, 1930, p. 197.
13. Kant, *Metaphysic of Morals*, 398.
14. H.J. Paton, 'Kant on Friendship', *Proceedings of the British Academy*, 1956.
15. Kant, *Metaphysic of Morals*, 402.
16. Kant, *Metaphysic of Morals*, 400.
17. R. Solomon, *The Passions*, p. 193. Garden City, NY., Anchor Press/ Doubleday, 1976.
18. Winch, 'Moral Integrity', pp. 12–13.
19. Kant, *Lectures on Ethics*, p. 199.
20. Mary Midgley, 'The Objection to Systematic Humbug', as reprinted in *Heart and Mind*, London, Methuen, 1981, p. 92.
21. Kant, *Lectures on Ethics*, p. 200.
22. Lewis Carroll, *Through the Looking Glass*, Harmondsworth, Puffin, 1962, p. 242.

23. Williams, 'Morality and the Emotions', p. 227.
24. Bertrand Russell, *Autobiography*.
25. Kant, *Lectures on Ethics*, p. 199.
26. As quoted in E. Cassirer, *Kant's Life and Thought*, New Haven, Conn., Yale University Press, 1981, p. 270.
27. This essay was first published in *Journal of Value Inquiry*, 1985, pp. 235–43.

Chapter 4 Time and Chance

1. Ecclesiastes, 9.11.
2. Although there are obviously large differences between the philosophers cited here, I place them together because they all reject central Kantian themes. See Alasdair MacIntyre, *After Virtue*, London, Duckworth, 1981; Martha Nussbaum, *The Fragility of Goodness*, Cambridge, Cambridge University Press, 1986; Richard Rorty, *Contingency, Irony and Solidarity*, Cambridge, Cambridge University Press, 1989, Bernard Williams, *Shame and Necessity*, Berkeley, University of California Press, 1993.
3. Rorty, *Contingency, Irony and Solidarity*, p. xiii.
4. The most famous exponent of this line of argument is Carol Gilligan, *In a Different Voice*, Cambridge, Mass., Harvard University Press, 1982.
5. Pindar, *Nemean*, VIII, 37–44, as quoted in Nussbaum, *The Fragility of Goodness*.
6. Percy Bysshe Shelley, *Prometheus Unbound*, III.iii.193.
7. Virginia Held, 'Liberty and Equality from a Feminist Perspective', in N. MacCormick and Z. Bankowski (eds) *Enlightenment, Rights and Revolution*, Aberdeen, Aberdeen University Press, 1989, p. 225.
8. Judith Shklar, *Ordinary Vices*, Cambridge, Mass., Harvard University Press, 1984, p. 233.
9. Rorty, *Contingency, Irony and Solidarity*, p. 34.
10. Rorty, *Contingency, Irony and Solidarity*, p. xvi.
11. Anne Philllips, 'Fraternity', in *Democracy and Difference*, Oxford and Cambridge, Polity, 1993, p. 35.
12. In L. Appignanesi and S. Maitland, *The Rushdie File*, London, Fourth Estate, 1989, p. 241.
13. Cheshire Calhoun, 'Justice, Care and Gender Bias', *Journal of Philosophy*, LXXXV, 1988, p. 456.
14. Immanuel Kant, *Lectures on Ethics*, London, Methuen, 1930, p. 197.
15. Ecclesiastes, 3.20.

Chapter 5 Marital Faithfulness

1. Thomas Hardy, *Jude The Obscure*, Harmondsworth, Penguin, 1978.
2. G.E. Moore, 'The Nature of Moral Philosophy', in *Philosophical Studies*, London, Routledge and Kegan Paul, 1922, p. 316.

3. Mary Midgley, 'The Objection to Systematic Humbug', *Philosophy*, Vol. 53, 1978, p. 147.
4. Bertrand Russell, *Autobiography*, London, George Allen and Unwin, 1967–9.
5. Derek Parfit, 'Later Selves and Moral Principles', in A. Montefiore (ed.) *Philosophy and Personal Relations*, London, Routledge, 1973, p. 144.
6. Parfit, 'Later Selves', p. 145.
7. Parfit, pp. 145–6.
8. Note 14, pp. 161–2.
9. Norman Malcolm, 'Knowledge and Belief', in A. Phillips Griffiths (ed.), *Knowledge and Belief*, Oxford, Oxford University Press, 1967, p. 81.
10. p. 78.
11. William Shakeaspeare, *A Midsummer Night's Dream*, Acts III and I.
12. W. Newton-Smith, 'A Conceptual Investigation of Love', in Montefiore (ed.) *Philosophy and Personal Relations*, pp. 132–3.
13. Alison Lurie, *Love and Friendship*, Harmondsworth, Penguin, 1962, pp. 329–30.
14. As quoted in John Casey, Actions and Consequences', in John Casey (ed.) *Morality and Moral Reasoning*, London, Methuen, 1971, p. 201.
15. Shakespeare, *Sonnets*, 91.
16. This essay was first published in *Philosophy*, Vol. 59, No. 228, 1984, pp. 243–52.

Chapter 6 To Have and To Hold: Liberalism and the Marriage Contract

1. Michael Sandel, *Liberalism and the Limits of Justice,* Cambridge, Cambridge University Press, 1982, p. 169.
2. Michael W. Jackson, *Matters of Justice*, Beckenham, Croom Helm, 1986, p. 3.
3. Jeremy Waldron, 'Theoretical Foundations of Liberalism', *Philosophical Quarterly*, 37, 1987, pp. 127–50.
4. Steven Lukes, *Individualism*, Oxford, Blackwell, 1973, p. 62.
5. As quoted in Waldron, 'Theoretical Foundations of Liberalism', p. 147.
6. Waldron, p. 147.
7. Carole Pateman, 'Feminist Critiques of the Public/Private Dichotomy', in Anne Phillips (ed.) *Feminism and Equality*, Oxford, Blackwell, 1987, p. 103.
8. Carole Pateman, 'The Shame of the Marriage Contract', in J. Stiehm (ed.) *Women's View of the Political World of Men*, pp. 80–1. New York, Transactional Publishers, Dubbs Ferry, 1984.
9. John Locke, 'Second Treatise of Government', in P. Laslett (ed.) *Two Treatises of Government,* Cambridge, Cambridge University Press, 1960, section 78.
10. Immanuel Kant, *Lectures on Ethics*, London, Methuen, 1979, p. 167.
11. Sandel, *Liberalism*, p. 106.

12. William Thompson, *Appeal on Behalf of One Half of the Human Race*, London, Virago, 1983, p. 55.
13. John Stuart Mill, *The Subjection of Women*, London, Virago, 1983, p. 55.
14. Pateman, 'The Shame of the Marriage Contract', M. Shanley, 'Marriage Contract and Social Contract in Seventeenth Century English Political Thought', *Western Political Quarterly*, XXXII, pp. 79–91.
15. Pateman, 'The Shame of the Marriage Contract', p. 78.
16. Sandel, *Liberalism*, p. 114.
17. For a fuller discussion of this, see my 'Liberty and Autonomy', *Proceedings of the Aristotelian Society*, LXXXVII, 1986/7, pp. 107–20.
18. Howard Williams, *Kant's Political Philosophy*, Oxford, Blackwell, 1983, p. 118.
19. Mill, *The Subjection of Women*, p. 177. Mill's views on marriage are more fully discussed in Essay 2 above.
20. Phyllis Rose, *Parallel Lives*, Harmondsworth, Penguin, 1985, pp. 15–16.
21. For a fuller discussion of unalterable commitment, see Chapter 5 above.
22. Bernard Williams, *Ethics and the Limits of Philosophy*, London, Fontana, 1985, p. 102.
23. This essay first appeared in *Archiv für Recht und SozialPhilosophie*, Vol. 36, 1988, pp. 46–53.

Chapter 7 Different Voices, Still Lives: Problems in the Ethics of Care

1. Carol Gilligan, *In A Different Voice*, Cambridge, Mass., Harvard University Press, 1982, pp. 159–60.
2. G.W.F. Hegel, *The Philosophy of Right*, trans. T.M. Knox, Oxford, Oxford University Press, 1952, p. 264.
3. J.J. Rousseau, *Emile, Œuvres Complètes de Jean-Jacques Rousseau*, IV, 693.
4. Anne Phillips, 'So What's Wrong with the Individual?', in Peter Osborne (ed.), *Socialism and the Limits of Liberalism*, London, Verso, 1991, p. 147.
5. Virginia Held, 'Liberty and Equality from a Feminist Perspective', in N. MacCormick and Z. Bankowski (eds) *Enlightenment, Rights and Revolution*, Aberdeen, Aberdeen University Press, 1989, p. 225.
6. Cheshire Calhoun, 'Justice, Care and Gender Bias', *Journal of Philosophy*, LXXXV (1988), p. 456.
7. Eva Feder Kittay and Diana T Meyers (eds), *Women and Moral Theory*, New York, Rowman and Littlefield, 1987, p. 10.
8. Held, 'Liberty and Equality', 225–6.
9. For a full discussion of this point, see Phillips, 'So What's Wrong with the Individual?'.
10. Mary Dietz, 'Citizenship with a Feminist Face: The Problem with Maternal Thinking', *Political Theory*, 13, 1985, p. 31.
11. David Miller, 'In What Sense must Socialism be Communitarian?', *Social Philosophy and Policy*, 5, 1989, pp. 66–7.
12. Michael Ignatieff, *The Needs of Strangers*, London, Hogarth, 1984, p. 42.

13. Phillips, 'So What's Wrong with the Individual?', p. 156.
14. As quoted in Gillian Parker, *With Due Care and Attention: A Review of Research on Informal Care*, London, Family Policy Studies Centre, 1985, p. 5.
15. Kittay and Meyers, *Women and Moral Theory*, p. 10.
16. Jean Elshtain, 'Antigone's Daughters', *Democracy*, 2, 1982, pp. 46–59. As quoted in Dietz, 'Citizenship with a Feminist Face'.
17. Dietz, 'Citizenship with a Feminist Face', p. 29.
18. David Miller has suggested to me that, in fact, Gilligan objects only to the conception of justice as a system of formal rules; not to the assumption of voluntariness in many theories of justice. His point draws attention to Gilligan's unwillingness to consider the possibility that there might be different conceptions of justice. I do not consider this here, but the point is admirably discussed by Andrew Mason in *Journal of the Theory of Social Behaviour*, 1990.
19. Michael Sandel, *Liberalism and the Limits of Justice*, Cambridge, Cambridge University Press, 1982, p. 179.
20. Chandran Kukathas and Philip Pettit, *Rawls: A Theory of Justice and its Critics*, Oxford and Cambridge, Polity, 1990, p. 109.
21. This essay was first published in *Journal of Applied Philosophy*, Vol. 19, No. 1, 1993, pp. 17–27.

Chapter 8 Tragedy, Moral Conflict and Liberalism

1. Steven Lukes, 'Making Sense of Moral Conflict', in Nancy Rosenblum (ed.) *Liberalism and the Moral Life*, Cambridge, Mass., Harvard University Press, 1989, p. 139.
2. John Stuart Mill, *On Liberty*, Harmondsworth, Penguin, 1978, p. 133.
3. Isaiah Berlin, 'Two Concepts of Liberty', in Berlin, *Four Essays on Liberty*, Oxford, Oxford University Press, 1969, p. 169.
4. Lukes, 'Making Sense of Moral Conflict', pp. 138–9.
5. Alasdair MacIntyre, *After Virtue*, London, Duckworth, 1981, p. 134.
6. John Rawls, *Political Liberalism*, New York, Columbia University Press, 1993, p. xvi.
7. Rawls, *Political Liberalism*, p. 139.
8. Brian Barry, *Justice as Impartiality*, Oxford, Oxford University Press, 1995, p. 251.
9. Rawls, *Political Liberalism*, p. 243, fn. 32.
10. Simon Caney, 'Anti-Perfectionism and Rawlsian Liberalism', *Political Studies*, 43, 1995, p. 256.
11. Arthur Miller, *The Theatre Essays of Arthur Miller*, London, Methuen, 1994, pp. 176–7.
12. Miller, *Theatre Essays*, p. 15.
13. John Rawls, *A Theory of Justice*, Oxford, Oxford University Press, 1972, p. 574. A full discussion of this aspect of Rawls's theory is provided in Chapter 11.

14. Judith Shklar, *The Faces of Injustice*, New Haven, Conn., Yale University Press, 1990, p. 57.
15. Shklar, *The Faces of Injustice*, p. 80.
16. Bernard Williams, *Shame and Necessity*, Berkeley, University of California Press, 1993, p. 125.
17. Shklar, *The Faces of Injustice*, pp. 79–80.
18. George Steiner, *The Death of Tragedy*, London, Faber, 1961, p. 353.
19. This essay was first published in David Archard (ed.), *Philosophy and Pluralism*, Cambridge, Cambridge University Press, 1996, pp. 191–201.

Chapter 9 Out of the Doll's House: Reflections on Autonomy and Political Philosophy

1. J.S. Mill, *On Liberty*, Penguin, Harmondsworth, 1974; John Rawls, *A Theory of Justice*, Oxford, University Press, 1971; Joseph Raz, *The Morality of Freedom*, Oxford, Clarendon Press, 1986.
2. Brian Barry, *Justice as Impartiality*, Oxford, Oxford University Press, 1995, p. 129.
3. Gerald Dworkin, 'The Concept of Autonomy', in John Christman, *The Inner Citadel: Essays on Individual Autonomy*, Oxford, Oxford University Press, 1989, pp. 54–5.
4. Isaiah Berlin, 'Two Concepts of Liberty', in *Four Essays on Liberty*, Oxford, University Press, 1969, p. 131.
5. Mill, *On Liberty*, p. 133.
6. Barry, *Justice as Impartiality*, p. 129.
7. Stanley Cavell, *Conditions Handsome and Unhandsome*, Illinois, Open Court, 1990.
8. Stephen Mulhall, 'Perfectionism, Politics and the Social Contract: Rawls and Cavell on Morality and Politics', *Journal of Political Philosophy*, Vol. 2, No. 3, 1994, pp. 222–39.
9. Alasdair MacIntyre, *After Virtue*, London, Duckworth, 1985 (second edition), p. 216.
10. Ibsen, *Doll's House*, Harmondsworth, Penguin, 1965, p. 226.
11. Ibsen, 'Notes for the Tragedy of Modern Times', in J.W. McFarlane (ed.) *The Oxford Ibsen*, London, Oxford University Press, 1961.
12. Michael Sandel, *Liberalism and the Limits of Justice*, Cambridge, Cambridge University Press, 1982.
13. This essay was originally published in *Philosophical Explorations*, Vol. 2, No. 1, January 1999, pp. 59–69.

Chapter 10 Strangers in Paradise: The Unhappy Marriage of Feminism and Conservatism

1. Margaret Atwood, *The Handmaid's Tale*, New York, Fawcett Crest, 1985, p. 164.

2. Katie Roiphe, *The Morning After*, London, Hamish Hamilton, 1993, p. 156.
3. Christine Bolt, *The Women's Movements in the United States and Britain from the 1790s to the 1920s*, Hemel Hempstead, Harvester, 1993, p. 130.
4. *The Women's Marements*, p. 132.
5. Carrie Chapman Catt, 'Do You Know', as quoted in M. Katzenstein and D. Laitin, 'Politics, Feminism, and the Ethics of Caring', in Eva Feder Kittay and Diana T. Meyers (eds) *Women and Moral Theory*, New York, Rowman and Littlefield, 1987, p. 266.
6. *Women and Moral Theory*, p. 268.
7. Roiphe, *The Morning After*, p. 156.
8. *The Morning After*, p. 160.
9. Katzenstein and Laitin, 'Politics, Feminism, and the Ethics of Caring', p. 271.
10. Michael Walzer, *Exodus and Revolution*, New York, Basic Books, 1985, p. 133.
11. *Exodus and Revolution*, p. 135.
12. Tom Moylan, *Demand the Impossible: Science Fiction and the Utopian Imagination*, London and New York, Methuen, 1986, p. 89.
13. *Demand the Impossible*, p. 101.
14. Elizabeth Frazer and Nicola Lacey, *The Politics of Community: A Feminist Critque of the Liberal-Communitarian Debate*, Hemel Hempstead, Harvester Wheatsheaf, 1993, p. 141.
15. Alison Jaggar, *Feminist Politics and Human Nature*, Brighton, Harvester, 1983, p. 97.
16. Catharine MacKinnon, *Towards a Feminist Theory of the State*, Cambridge, Mass., Harvard University Press, 1989, p. 135.
17. Carole Pateman, *The Sexual Contract*, Oxford and Cambridge, Polity, 1988, p. 108.
18. Isaiah 65:21–2.
19. Micah 4:4.
20. Ronald Dworkin, 'Only Words', *New York Review of Books*, 3 March 1994, p. 48.
21. Catharine MacKinnon, 'Pornography, Civil Rights and Speech', in Catherine Itzin (ed.) *Pornography: Women, Violence and Civil Liberties*, Oxford, Oxford University Press, 1992, p. 461.

Chapter 11 The Importance of Love in Rawls's Theory of Justice

1. I am very grateful to Derek Bell, Simon Caney, Peter Jones and Matt Matravers for extensive help with this chapter.
2. David Hume, *A Treatise of Human Nature*, Oxford, Clarendon Press, 1888, p. 497.
3. John Rawls, *A Theory of Justice*, Oxford, Oxford University Press, 1972, p. 573.
4. Rawls, *A Theory of Justice*, p. 573.

5. John Rawls, *Political Liberalism*, New Haven, Conn., Columbia University Press, 1993, p. xviii.
6. Rawls, *Political Liberalism*, p. 142.
7. Rawls, *A Theory of Justice*, p. 454.
8. Rawls, *A Theory of Justice*, p. 477.
9. Rawls, *A Theory of Justice*, p. 476.
10. Brian Barry, 'John Rawls and the Search for Stability', *Ethics*, 105, 1995, 874–915, p. 885.
11. Rawls, *A Theory of Justice*, pp. 477–8.
12. Jonathan Dancy, 'Intuitionism', in Peter Singer (ed.) *A Companion to Ethics*, Oxford, Blackwell, 1993, pp. 411–20, p. 414.
13. I am grateful to Simon Caney for drawing my attention to this ambiguity, and to Matt Matravers for discussion of it. They are not responsible for the claims I make here.
14. This formulation appeared originally in T.M. Scanlon, 'Contractualism and Utilitarianism', in Amartya Sen and Bernard Williams (eds) *Utilitarianism and Beyond*, Cambridge, Cambridge University Press, 1982, p. 116.
15. Barry, 'John Rawls and the Search for Stability', p. 884.
16. Rawls, *A Theory of Justice*, p. 567.
17. Rawls, *A Theory of Justice*, p. 568.
18. Barry, 'John Rawls and the Search for Stability', p. 889.
19. Scanlon, 'Contractualism and Utilitarianism', p. 105.
20. Rawls, *A Theory of Justice*, p. 573.
21. Immanuel Kant, *The Doctrine of Virtue: Part II of the Metaphysic of Morals*, trans. Mary Gregor, Philadelphia, University of Pennsylvania Press, 1964, p. 116.
22. Kant, *Metaphysic of Morals*, pp. 142–3.
23. Immanuel Kant, *Lectures on Ethics*, trans. Louis Infield, London, Methuen and Co., 1979, p. 208.
24. Charles Fried, *An Anatomy of Values: Problems of Personal and Social Choice*, Harvard, Mass., Harvard University Press, 1970, p. 79. I am grateful to Tom Baldwin for drawing my attention to this argument in Fried.
25. Michael J. Sandel, *Liberalism and the Limits of Justice*, Cambridge, Cambridge University Press, 1982, p. 183.
26. Scanlon, 'Contractualism and Utilitarianism', p. 105.
27. Barry, 'John Rawls and the Search for Stability', p. 889.
28. These points draw upon Martin Hollis, 'The Shape of a Life', in J.E.J. Altham and Ross Harrison (eds) *World, Mind and Ethics: Essays on the Ethical Philosophy of Bernard Williams*, Cambridge, Cambridge University Press, 1995, pp. 170–84.
29. Scanlon, 'Contractualism and Utilitarianism', p. 116.
30. Harry Frankfurt, 'The Importance of What We Care About', in *The Importance of What We Care About*, Cambridge, Cambridge University Press, 1988, pp. 80–94, pp. 89–90. I am grateful to Frank Crawley for introducing me to this piece and for helpful discussions of the arguments in it.
31. Frankfurt, 'The Importance of What We Care About', pp. 90–1.
32. Rawls, *A Theory of Justice*, pp. 574–5.

33. Rawls, *A Theory of Justice*, p. 575.
34. Rawls, *Political Liberalism*, p. 143.
35. Brian Barry falls into this camp. See 'John Rawls and the Search for Stability'. This essay was first published in *British Journal of Political Science*, January 1999.

Index